THE 10 KEYS OF

EFFECTIVE
SUPERVISION

THE 10 KEYS OF

EFFECTIVE
SUPERVISION

Building Healthy Organizational Cultures
through Servant Leadership

RICK PIERCE & JIM ROWELL

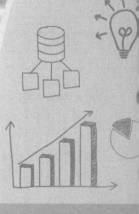

Advantage

Published by Advantage, Charleston, South Carolina.
Member of Advantage Media Group.

ADVANTAGE is a registered trademark, and the Advantage colophon is a trademark of Advantage Media Group, Inc.

Printed in the United States of America.

10 9 8 7 6 5 4 3 2 1

ISBN: 978-1-59932-828-7
LCCN: 2017932798

Cover design by Katie Biondo.

This publication is designed to provide accurate and authoritative information in regard to the subject matter covered. It is sold with the understanding that the publisher is not engaged in rendering legal, accounting, or other professional services. If legal advice or other expert assistance is required, the services of a competent professional person should be sought.

Advantage Media Group is proud to be a part of the Tree Neutral® program. Tree Neutral offsets the number of trees consumed in the production and printing of this book by taking proactive steps such as planting trees in direct proportion to the number of trees used to print books. To learn more about Tree Neutral, please visit **www.treeneutral.com.**

Advantage Media Group is a publisher of business, self-improvement, and professional development books. We help entrepreneurs, business leaders, and professionals share their Stories, Passion, and Knowledge to help others Learn & Grow. Do you have a manuscript or book idea that you would like us to consider for publishing? Please visit **advantagefamily.com** or call **1.866.775.1696.**

This book is dedicated to the honor and glory of God and to those individuals committed to the joy of servant leadership!

TABLE OF CONTENTS

FOREWORD

What characterizes a leader you will trust and follow?

Too many leaders don't know the answer to that question—or they haven't internalized it in their own beliefs and behavior. In this wonderful book, you will find 10 Keys that will help you unlock the answers to being the kind of leader you would be willing to follow.

Much of my professional work and personal calling has been in the domain of helping people gain credibility and behave in ways that inspire trust—as a person, as a leader, as a contributor in a community. High-trust leaders possess the same intent servant leaders do—purely and simply to serve others—coworkers, customers, partners, communities. Your intent—your motive, your agenda—may be intangible and invisible. But don't think for a moment that it is hidden. People sense it and feel it in everything you say and do.

The servant leader is motivated by caring, and the agenda she seeks is mutual benefit: "Yes, I want to win, but it is equally important to me (and perhaps even more important) that you win." I have worked with plenty of servant leaders and smart supervisors. When their intent was pure, I knew it. And I never needed to second-guess their agenda or motive. And, significantly, I wanted to give them my best in terms of quality work and personal loyalty. They truly inspired me to perform better, and they absolutely brought out the best in me. As Cheryl Bachelder, CEO of Popeye's Louisiana Kitchen and one of the world's great servant leaders today, stated, "All truly great leaders are servant leaders because they serve the people well—and the followers know the difference."

But why wait for people to infer your intent? You can accelerate trust by declaring your intent.

The intent of the authors of *The 10 Keys of Effective Supervision* is to equip you with the practical thinking, tools, and tips that will help you become a better servant leader and supervisor. This book does so admirably. I believe Rick Pierce and Jim Rowell have made a significant contribution to the applied fields of both servant leadership and effective supervision. Like my father, the late Dr. Stephen R. Covey, I have been a long-time advocate of the principles of servant leadership and this book is a must-read for anyone serving others in a leadership role.

How does it do so? Through simple structures that transform conceptual ideas to practical actions any leader can take. You'll find this book an easy read. Each chapter begins with an engaging story of a coach from a summer camp that illustrates the concept that follows. And each of those chapters is structured by the ingenious acronym "SUPERVISOR" that helps you remember—and turn—the 10 Keys they have identified in effective servant leaders.

By the end of the book, you will know that although servant leadership is not necessarily always the easiest route to take, it is always the right route to take. Treating people with dignity and respect, building people up rather than tearing them down, and leading from your intent rather from your position absolutely pays off in ways you can't even imagine yet.

My congratulations to Rick and Jim on an excellent book that is both insightful and practical. I trust it will help you in your journey of helping people as a servant leader!

—Stephen M. R. Covey

Author of The New York Times *bestseller,* The Speed of Trust, *and former President & CEO of Covey Leadership Center*

ACKNOWLEDGMENTS

First, we would like to acknowledge God in providing the first Servant Leader and giving us the wisdom and strength to share His picture of positive leadership.

Next, we would like to thank our families, without whose constant patience, love, support, and sacrifice neither Rising Sun Consultants, nor this book, could ever have been possible:

- Jayne, Alexis, Samantha, and Tom (Elerowski) Pierce

- Diane, Danielle, Benjamin, Rebecca, and Emily Rowell

We would also like to thank the following three individuals for their input, comments, and support on the initial version of this book and the development of the 10 Keys model:

- Lynn Tonini

- Kim Garosi

- Dennette Moul

We would like to thank all the members of the copy, editorial, and design teams at Advantage—particularly Bob Sheasley, Alex Rogers, Katie Biondo, Megan Elger, and Nate Best for their constant advice, support, and encouragement throughout this process.

We would like to offer special thanks to Dr. John Covey for his continuous love and support throughout our years of friendship.

We would especially like to thank Stephen Covey for his kind words and support for this project and for writing the foreword for the book.

Finally, we would also like to thank all of our supervisors, mentors, and clients who have helped teach us the importance and meaning behind serving others and leading with a servant's heart.

A WORD FROM THE AUTHORS

RICK PIERCE

I have been very lucky to have had a unique and diverse career. My experiences have ranged from college professor to small business owner to executive leader to international consultant. When I was in my midforties, I was given what I thought was the opportunity of a lifetime—I was hired for a senior leadership position at one of the largest nonprofit homes/schools for disadvantaged youth anywhere in the world. It was there that I met my friend, coauthor, and business partner, Jim Rowell.

An extremely wealthy organization serving disadvantaged youth in the middle of Central Pennsylvania—what could go wrong? What I quickly learned was that lots of money, a powerful mission, and beautiful surroundings meant very little if I didn't have the knowledge and skills I needed to create a healthy organizational culture.

When I was first hired at the school, a new organizational chart was issued naming me as the new dean. Right there at the top of the chart, in bold letters, it said "Richard A. Pierce, PhD—Dean." My ego was on fire.

However, I soon learned that it meant nothing if the rest of the names on the chart didn't feel valued and supported. After reading an article on servant leadership, I asked my administrative assistant to redo the chart, putting me at the bottom. Just above my name, we listed my direct reports. Above them were the frontline administrators and above them the houseparents who directly cared for the kids. Finally, at the top of the chart, where I used to reside, were the students. After all, the kids were what the school was all about. I then asked my assistant to put a graphic of a pair of hands around the chart to illustrate the idea of support from the bottom of the chart to the top.

That upside-down approach, as it turned out, was really the right-side-up approach. The gesture pleased many of the staff and led to my lifelong study of, and commitment to, the principles of servant leadership. My desire has always been to help and to serve others. I wanted that to be the nature of my life's work. Wherever I worked, I wanted to wake up eager and grateful for the privilege of being there. What I have learned through the years is that the relationships within a company can be even more meaningful than the work itself.

A strong, clear culture is what makes a company great. In such a culture, the employees will serve the organization loyally—and not because they must do it but because they want to do it. As my career evolved, I kept asking myself these questions as a supervisor: *How can we do this better? How can we treat people so that they want to come to work? How would I like to have me as a supervisor?*

Many organizations find themselves experiencing high turnover rates, and research suggests that most people are not leaving because they will be getting more money but rather because they are fleeing a poor relationship with a supervisor. With this in mind, we write this book primarily to the middle managers or supervisors, the ones who directly supervise the workers.

Good relationships with employees engender both loyalty and productivity. That is why supervisors should care about what we are communicating in this book. Treating their employees with dignity and respect and value will make a huge difference in their lives—not only will it be the right thing to do but they will also be helping the bottom line.

Every chapter of this book begins with a few paragraphs about a man I'll call "Coach." As you read about this man, understand that the portrait created about him combines the observations and experiences of many people who knew him—including me.

Coach was the head counselor of a boys' camp in the Pocono Mountains region of Pennsylvania. His life lessons always meant a lot to me, as well as to many others who knew him. It was from him that I learned much of what I know about strong supervision and leadership. Coach knew instinctively how to use the Keys that we will examine in this book, and, as you will see, he put them into action on a daily basis there at the summer camp in the mountains.

JIM ROWELL

Since I was nineteen, when I was a resident assistant at my college, I have had supervisory and leadership roles. Later, I worked a position where employees were unionized and complained constantly about what they perceived to be miserable conditions. They would come to me daily asking for help because they were being treated poorly. Through such experiences, I developed a deep caring for the well-being of people.

For years, the statistics have been consistent. About three quarters of employees across the country are unhappy where they work. They don't feel that their employer cares about them or values them. I strongly believe that it need not be that way. Much of our life is spent in the workplace. For anyone to be laboring in misery is a shame, and countless organizations have a great opportunity to do better. With a change of heart and an assortment of skills, they can develop a dedicated, enthusiastic, and productive workforce.

That is the goal for the business that Rick and I launched, and it is the goal of this book. We wrote this for the frontline supervisors, managers, directors, line leaders, crew leaders, and others in such roles. Company executives should see the value and benefits for their supervisors and managers within these pages. However, it is the middle managers and supervisors who have the greatest impact on people's lives, and that is the group we wish to influence.

It's all about value and dignity. I believe from a spiritual perspective that we need to care for people and treat them well. It can be difficult. In the workplace and in families, individuals can be quarrelsome and their behavior can be hard to tolerate. That doesn't mean we can ever treat them badly. Good leaders preserve the spirit of dignity even when people get upset.

Supervisors who observe the 10 Keys within this book on a daily basis will see the growth of productivity and success. Their employees will stick around longer, work harder, waste less, and show up regularly and on time. Such are the dividends of treating people well.

"As many small trickles of water feed the mightiest of rivers, the growing number of individuals and organizations practicing servant leadership has increased into a torrent, one that carries with it a deep current of meaning and passion."

— LARRY SPEARS

A SERVANT'S HEART

As he drove home alone from the funeral, his thoughts turned toward the wonderful memories he had of "Coach," who had been his mentor for the past twenty summers at a boys camp in the Pocono Mountains of Pennsylvania. Coach had supervised him and the other counselors there, teaching them the value of respecting others and respecting themselves.

Coach was a humble soul—not self-effacing but humble in the true sense of the word: he cared for others, and he put their needs ahead of his own, striving to build them up without tearing himself down. Over the years, Coach emphasized that the most essential ingredient to successful leadership and supervision was to have a servant's heart. He cared deeply about everyone he worked with, both personally and professionally.

Driving over the Delaware River after Coach's funeral, he recalled a time many years earlier when a younger version of himself had crossed that bridge on a bus going to the camp for the first time. He was nineteen and had just finished his freshman year at college and was about to spend the next two months at the camp, one of the most respected in the Poconos. Little did he know how the experience would shape the rest of his life.

Working at the camp over the next two decades, he would learn many important lessons in both effective leadership and supervision from this natural servant leader. Although he had an amazing presence and self-confidence, Coach was not a man with a big ego. In fact, he recalled how that first summer, Coach had worked hard to develop a new program for the kids, but the owner of the camp shot down the idea. Coach just smiled graciously. The following week, the owner announced a great new initiative and proceeded to take credit for Coach's idea, word for word. Again, Coach just smiled and expressed his support.

"It's not about who gets the recognition," he later explained when a group of counselors complained about how unfairly he had been treated. "It's all about what's best for the kids."

At the manufacturing company where he was employed, Joe was the first to arrive and the last to leave. Not only was he proficient at his own job but he also could do the work of those around him when necessary—and do it well.

Joe's managers soon noticed this hard-working young man and figured he deserved a promotion. They turned him into a supervisor. However, Joe was soon struggling. His people complained about how he treated them, and he got grumpier as morale declined. The managers wondered what had happened to their star employee. He had been doing a great job, and now he had a sour attitude and was alienating the staff.

That's when the company asked our firm, Rising Sun Consultants, to come in. We started giving Joe one-on-one coaching around our "10 Keys of Effective Supervision" program that this book is based on. Joe came to see that despite his technical proficiency and his strong work ethic, he had not developed the skills to deal well with people in a way that preserved their sense of dignity and value. He had regarded people much like the machinery they operated. His attitude was: "Just do what I need you to do when I tell you to do it." He had never had trouble getting metal and bolts to do his bidding. Flesh and blood was a different matter.

After working with us weekly for several months, Joe had a dramatic change in his approach. He reached out to his people, spending time with them and regularly asking them each how they were doing. He asked them not just about their jobs but also about their lives and families. He began to restore positive relationships. Joe's managers were thrilled with this turnaround, and the people he supervised certainly noticed the change. Joe still works at that company.

Several months after his sessions with us concluded, Joe stopped by to say hello and mentioned that he had experienced a big difference in his home life, as well. The new focus on value and dignity was transforming his personal relationships. His wife and children were interacting with him more positively. His career coaching had enriched his life beyond the workplace.

All too often, organizations promote employees based solely on their strong technical or clinical experience. Effective supervisors, however, have another enormous responsibility: they must also be good coaches. They must know how to bring out the best in others.

Most people, at some point in their working lives, have resigned or asked for a transfer—or at least thought about it—because they were fed up with a supervisor who seemed to lack the human touch.

As a result, many employers consistently report high turnover, which costs our economy billions of dollars each year.

Those surly supervisors hurt the bottom line. Depending on the industry, the cost of turnover typically is reported as about the same as the employee's yearly salary plus benefits. According to the Gallup Organization, most employees who resign cite dissatisfaction with the job duties, the culture, the manager, or the work environment. They often feel that they are not valued. Many describe themselves as either disengaged or actively disengaged. No longer can supervisors point at anyone but themselves as the primary cause of turnover and employee dissatisfaction.

This book is written primarily for the middle managers or supervisors, those who have so much influence over the prevailing morale in any organization. At Rising Sun Consultants, we do our best to help organizations and the individuals within them confront such problems and battle that trend. Over the years, we have developed a set of strategies that we call "The 10 Keys of Effective Supervision." In this book, we have organized those Keys into chapters. As a convenient way to help our readers commit those principles to memory, the first letter of each Key will spell the word "supervisor."

Here are the 10 Keys, which we will examine chapter by chapter:

1. **S** upporting Growth—Providing support for employees' personal and professional development.

2. **U** niting Your Team—Building a culture of care and concern among and between employees.

3. **P** raising Others—Offering employees praise and encouragement and developing a motivational environment.

4. **E** xpecting Excellence—Setting high expectations for employees.

5. **R** equiring Accountability—Upholding and reinforcing individual responsibility to the organization.

6. **V** aluing What You Believe—Linking employees' actions and behaviors to organizational values—building a healthy culture.

7. **I** nstilling Independence—Developing an atmosphere of hope, confidence, and autonomy.

8. **S** haring Continuously—Establishing open and honest two-way communication.

9. **O** ptimizing Ownership—Creating opportunities for employee contribution and buy-in.

10. **R** ealigning Your Efforts—Evaluating your own efforts to determine if they match your desired outcomes.

Please note that although we have grouped the 10 Keys to spell "supervisor," they are all of equal importance. However, although all are necessary for success, they need not be applied in any particular order. In addition, any one of these Keys can be underused or overused and can lead to potential problems. For example, if you only address an employee's lack of performance and never provide positive feedback, then you risk creating a "gotcha" culture. Some supervisors only look to catch what employees do wrong, rather than acknowledging their successes. Yes, it is important to hold people accountable, but it is just as important to reinforce what they do right through positive praise and encouragement.

Effective supervision will go a long way toward promoting increased productivity, employee engagement, and a healthy organizational culture. Improving on supervision is an essential strategy for influencing overall organizational success. We have observed, however, that many supervisors don't believe that this aspect of their role is important. They want to be left alone to do their job. They don't believe that taking care of others should be their first responsibility. However, given the chance to work with supervisors, we have been able to demonstrate that treating employees right will increase productivity by improving morale. They see the practical side of figuring out how to deal with people.

The 10 Keys of Effective Supervision: Building Healthy Organizational Cultures through Servant Leadership is the culmination of more than a decade of study and research involving our clients as well as the hundreds of people who have attended our seminars and workshops on the 10 Keys. The 10 Keys approach differs from that used by many organizations. We see supervision as having more to do with coaching and mentoring than strictly instruction and accountability. From our perspective, the supervisor's role should have less to do with teaching and evaluation and more to do with establishing a culture that encourages individual growth and development.

Supervisors who develop in themselves the characteristics that we will examine in this book will see a change in their lifestyle that transcends the workplace. It's a change from the inward "me" focus to the outward focus on "other." Life becomes more about serving the needs of others rather than having others serve you.

LEADING WITH A SERVANT'S HEART

The concept of servant leadership has blossomed in workplaces far and wide over the past four decades as organizations compete to retain qualified and committed employees. Robert Greenleaf formalized the term as a leadership method in 1970. Greenleaf, an expert in management research, development, and education was consultant to AT&T, the Ford Foundation, and other large organizations. For much of his career, he advocated the benefits of leadership through serving others.

Greenleaf called servant leadership "a practical philosophy that supports people who choose to serve first and then lead as a way of expanding service to individuals and institutions."[1] Every organization exists for those it serves. The people who usually are placed at the bottom of the organizational chart are the ones who will make or break it. No leader, no matter how great, can excel without good employees who care about the customers or the clients. Without that strength, and without that sense of priority, the organization will fail.

Several other prominent authors have expanded on the concept of servant leadership. Ken Blanchard addresses it in his book *The*

---

1   Robert Greenleaf, K., *Servant Leadership* (Mahwah, NJ: Paulist Press, 1977).

Secret: What Great Leaders Know and Do, offering insights into how servant leadership can be achieved. The organizational strategist Peter Senge says that "leadership is a social process, something that happens between people."[2] Senge suggests that leaders can improve their organizations by investing in building relationships, such as those formed through servant leadership.

Many organizations have been evolving to favor humanistic approaches to leadership over authoritarian ones. In his book *Good to Great,* Jim Collins says a principal difference between good organizations and great ones is what he calls "Level 5 leadership." A leader at that level, he says, is characterized by humility and tenacity, similar to how Greenleaf and others describe the servant leader. Higher education also has embraced the concept. Several leading universities, such as Harvard Business School, have adapted servant leadership training into their curriculums.

This is not to say that servant leadership is a modern concept. It's an ancient one. The Bible clearly addresses it: "Whoever wants to become great among you must be your servant, and whoever wants to be first must be your slave—just as the Son of Man did not come to be served, but to serve, and to give his life as a ransom for many" (Matthew 20:26–28). God's people, says Ephesians 4:12, are equipped "for works of service." Something old has become something new.

So what are the traits of servant leadership? Greenleaf and others describe it as a style that encourages collaboration, persuasion, trust, and listening. It is characterized by foresight, empowerment, and awareness, and it promotes healing and empathy. It aims for stewardship and building of community.

---

2   Peter M. Senge, *The Fifth Disciple: The Art & Practice of Learning Organizations,* (Doubleday, 2006).

By practicing those traits, servant leaders experience a personal transformation that extends beyond the organization. Their leadership style becomes their worldview, a way of living. They may or may not hold formal positions of leadership. What makes them servant leaders is not their rank but rather how they treat people, whether on the job, at home, or in the community.

The formal leader will not necessarily be the one to whom people go when they are looking for direction. They will take their questions and their gripes to the one with whom they have built a relationship, whether or not that is their supervisor. It is our hope and aim that the designated supervisors can build the kind of trusting relationship through servant leadership that will attract the staff to come to them for answers.

Unfortunately, many supervisors instead use power for leverage. Imagine that your supervisor gives you a task and tells you how to do it. Based on your years of experience, you offer an alternative strategy. "If you want to keep your job, do it my way!" the supervisor says. How would you feel? Now, imagine your supervisor assigns you a task, asks your opinion on how to do it, and gives you the autonomy to do as you suggested. Now how would you feel? Which supervisor would make you feel valued and motivated? Whose style would make you want to look for another job?

RISING TO THE CHALLENGES

Servant leadership does not come without challenges. Leaders must be flexible, for many reasons. They may possess the traits of servant leadership, but what matters is how they use those traits. How do they adapt and interact with those they lead? Servant leaders should reflect on their experiences and learn from them, for the betterment of themselves and the betterment of the organization.

It's hard enough to change your own worldview regarding leadership, and it is certainly no easy task to influence others to do so. Many organizations, however, have successfully overcome the challenges as they have adopted the strategy of servant leadership.

OPERATING IN THE RIGHT ZONE

At Rising Sun Consultants, we believe that the success of an organization, and of its individual employees, can best be viewed through the three lenses of competency, commitment, and character. Where all three lenses overlap is the realm of excellence that we call the ProductivityZone™.

Employee productivity traditionally has been measured by knowledge and skills, which is the lens of competency, and by attitude, which is the lens of commitment. We take the study of productivity a step further. We add the lens of character, which focuses on morals and values.

As can be seen in the illustration, any two of these zones alone are insufficient for true excellence and high productivity. Employees with character and competence, for example, may still feel disengaged in their job. Those with character and commitment may be likable sorts who just don't have the skills to get the job done. And you might have competent people on your staff who are committed to sticking around—but you might be better off if they left because they might not share your values.

The bottom line is productivity. Organizations exist to get things done. The objective is growth. If organizations are to thrive, they need the right kind of employees and the right kind of supervisors to lead them. We encourage you to keep the lenses on the top of your mind as you continue through the chapters of this book and explore the "10 Keys to Effective Supervision." These three lenses, properly focused, provide a clear view of excellence in any organization.

High Potential, Disengaged People

Qualified, Inconsistent People

Competency
(knowledge & skills)

Productivity Zone

Character
(morals & values)

Commitment
(engagement)

Well Intended, Ineffective People

"Servant leadership requires a level of intimacy with the needs and aspirations of the people being led that might be beyond the level of intimacy an ego-driven leader is willing to sustain."

— KEN BLANCHARD

CHAPTER 1

SUPPORTING GROWTH

Every summer, as the bus made its way down the tree-lined dirt road past the cottages, ball fields, and well-groomed grounds, Coach waited in front of the main building to greet the counselors he had hired. In his many years coaching high school basketball, he had become the consummate educator and mentor. He saw to it that others were successful, whether on the basketball court or at the camp he so dearly loved. He was ready to play that role once again with the new arrivals.

The owner of the camp welcomed the group and then turned the meeting over to Coach, who spoke with gentle confidence about the mission, vision, and values of the camp. He focused on their responsibilities to the "young men" (ages four to sixteen) whom the counselors would be "serving" for the ensuing eight weeks. Coach made it clear to the group why they were there and what was expected.

From that day forward, he guided and supported each and every counselor. He regularly challenged them to consider how their actions were in line with the mission of serving the kids. He never told the counselors what to do or how to do it, though. Instead, he helped them look for alternatives and supported them as they made their decisions.

Bob was the best widget maker the company had ever hired. It was as if he lived and breathed to make those widgets, and his handiwork stood out as superior. In fact, he was so much faster and so much better than his comrades that the company managers began to wonder whether the other widget makers were slacking off. Perhaps somebody who knew a good widget when he saw one should come in and help improve production and quality.

"Congratulations, Bob, we are giving you a promotion," the managers told him. "We're going to give you a break from making widgets so that you can show the others just what they should be doing. They need someone to keep them on their toes. They need someone like you."

Bob was a humble and gentle soul, however, and not the whip-cracking type. He aimed to please, not to confront. That's why he was so good at making widgets—he wanted the managers to be happy with him. He wanted everyone to be happy with him. He didn't want to disappoint anyone. So, of course, he never said a word suggesting he might not want the promotion and didn't want to be a supervisor, and the managers never asked him.

Bob soon became a dismal failure at his job. The other widget makers saw him as a pushover, and they began showing up late, taking two-hour lunch breaks, and making increasingly poor-quality widgets. Once in a while, Bob would suggest that he would prefer they not do things that way, but they paid no attention to him. He began to wish he had never seen a widget.

It was a setup for failure. Bob was cast into a role for which he was temperamentally unsuited and woefully untrained. Instead of looking carefully at Bob's strengths and talents, the managers had made presumptions that jeopardized his career and livelihood. They failed to support his personal and professional growth.

Supporting growth is an essential responsibility for all managers and supervisors. They must pay attention to the professional and personal development of employees they supervise. Nothing is more important to the success of an organization than the quality and professionalism of its staff. To create a professional staff, you need more than just a hiring process, or just a training program. You need a comprehensive perspective. All too often, organizations deal with professional development by tackling issues narrowly. Instead, they need a holistic or systems approach.

A CULTURE OF LIFELONG LEARNING

For a professional development program to be truly effective, the organization must instill a strong emphasis throughout its ranks on the value of learning—and that learning must be directly related to what the organization is striving to do or produce.

For example, if the focus of the organization is human services, then the training should be people oriented. If the organization is product oriented, then the training should focus on how to get that product to market and how to get people to buy it. Even if the training will be on techniques of leadership and supervision, it still should be geared toward the fundamental nature of what the organization does.

The organization's cultural environment should advance and encourage lifelong learning. Employees tend to see training as punishment rather than as a gift from the organization to help them grow and develop. To fight that tendency, the leadership should serve as a model of enthusiasm for such training. They should communicate the opportunity for everyone to learn to excel in making the company more marketable—as well as the individuals working for it.

From our point of view, a professional development program needs to be sustained, systemic, and systematic. Let's take a look at each of those qualities. Ask yourself whether your organization's program meets these criteria:

- A "sustained" professional development program is continuous. Professional development is not a single event but a series of related learning opportunities that support individual growth and organizational success.

- A "systemic" professional development program plays a critical role throughout an organization's culture. The focus of learning opportunities does not change depending on who is responsible for professional development. The training remains consistent and is integrated in all aspects of the organization.

- A "systematic" professional development program is developed and implemented methodically and intentionally. It is aligned with the mission, vision, and guiding principles of the organization. Systematic programs provide consistent themes across all work groups, while providing support for specific departments and individual needs.

COACHING FOR GROWTH

Servant leaders look beyond the workplace to see staff members as individuals with specific needs. By helping each employee to grow both on the job and off the job, the organization also reaps the benefits.

To that end, coaching and mentoring are valuable tools. Effective supervisors act as coaches to encourage employees to learn and be challenged by their work. They help the employees to define goals and objectives, both for themselves and for the organization.

The focus of that coaching should be on the accomplishments of the present and future, not solely on examining past mistakes. A healthy coaching environment will encourage wise risk taking and consider those mistakes to be opportunities to learn and develop.

We recently worked with a senior leader who had read extensively about servant leadership but did not know how to apply it. He made the classic mistake of thinking that servant leaders were soft. Over the course of several months, he grew impressively as a leader. He has become a very active servant leader rather than a passive one. He has made it clear to his reports, for example, that he will solicit and value their collaboration but that he sometimes will be making the decisions to keep things moving forward. When we first began working with him, he never would have said something like that. He would have wallowed in indecision.

His personal growth clearly will feed into the organization's success, and that is the value of creating a learning community. Such a learning community can evolve through strategies such as orientation training, use of professional development plans, strength-based performance appraisal systems, tuition reimbursement for continuing education, increased involvement in committees, increased involvement in professional associations, writing for newsletters or journals, and providing opportunities for advancement. Those are all valuable means by which supervisors can support growth.

It is the individual coaching, though, that will take performance improvement to the next level. Coaching is an art. It closes the gap between how things are and how they should be. The coach and employee take stock in the current situation and then identify the goals and desired outcomes. Together, they brainstorm strategies and implement them. Then they assess the results, and they keep on trying and refining in their quest for ever-greater improvement.

GROOMING YOUR BEST PEOPLE

We once worked with a tire manufacturer that was so well respected in the industry that its competitors would recruit their employees. Its reputation for quality training was so good that the other tire makers figured that even its castoffs might be better than what they had. That's an unusual approach to professional development, yes, but it powerfully illustrates the importance of a good training program.

Many companies have been losing a fifth to a quarter of their employees annually. The cost of hiring is no chump change. You have to advertise. You have to pore over those resumes. You spend time and energy conducting those interviews. Perhaps you pay the candidates' travel and relocation expenses. And then you invest several months into training to get the new hire up to speed. The whole time, the job has either been completed or other employees have had to do the extra work. Such is the cost of turnover.

By investing time, attention, and professional development dollars in your top people, you reduce the likelihood that they will leave for "greener pastures." When you continue to challenge and reward talented employees, you eliminate their need to seek opportunities elsewhere. When some do leave, though, your company's reputation will grow if other employers see the quality of your people. In that way, those training dollars translate to public relations dollars.

And if you applaud all efforts to advance professionally, whether with you or elsewhere, then you will have raging fans for life.

However, if an employee is fundamentally unsuited for a job or for a promotion, no amount of coaching and training is likely to change matters. As an essential step in the long-term success of any organization, servant leaders must have the courage to decide who will be the best choice for advancement. Supervisors need to match up the organization's future needs with the skills and aspirations of individual employees.

That requires a conscious system of succession planning. A successful system will consider both what is in the best interest of the organization and what is in the best interest of those who work for it. As was the case with poor Bob the widget maker, forcing employees onto job tracks that they don't want or that do not match their skills and inclinations can cause damage all around, corporately and individually. As a supervisor, you must determine where the employee wants to be, what he or she wants to do, and whether that fits the organization's needs.

Here are some things you can do to support growth:

- Develop a strength-based performance appraisal system.

- Offer tuition reimbursement.

- Use your staff's expertise for training purposes.

- Encourage staff to step outside their comfort zone.

- Offer meetings and seminars for cross-training.

- Encourage participation in industry conferences and associations.

- Share industry trends and concepts with all employees.

- Invest significantly in coaching and training.

- Develop a training library specific to your organization.

- Provide opportunities for advancement.

Applying the principles:

- Select an appropriate employee.

- Determine why this employee needs coaching.

- Determine the employee's present reality.

- Determine the desired outcome.

- List possible strategies to support the employee's growth.

- Implement coaching.

- Assess progress and growth toward the desired outcome.

"Good teams become great ones when the members trust each other enough to surrender the 'me' for the 'we.'"

—PHIL JACKSON

CHAPTER 2

UNITING YOUR TEAM

Coach always tried to make sure that the camp counselors got along and worked well as a team. He began each meeting by having the counselors share things about themselves or about the "good things" they had seen another counselor do. He often had them play games or solve puzzles requiring them to interact.

At one meeting that first summer, Coach broke the group into pairs for a scavenger hunt to learn more about the camp. The counselors, not seeing the point, didn't put much effort into the exercise. The next week, Coach sent them out again—but this time, the pair who finished first would get an extra afternoon "off duty." The results were quite different—and the most successful teams were the ones that divided the work and communicated best.

The counselors at first wondered why Coach cared how they got along. After all, they were there for the kids, not for one another. However, as time passed, it started to make sense. Coach was creating his "team." The importance came to light one day that summer when a counselor and two campers got lost on a nature hike. The team pulled together to find their comrade and the campers.

> *Coach taught the group that regardless of the task, if people are to work together successfully, then they must transition from a "group" of individuals into a collaborative "team."*

The training director at the organization where we once worked together was scheduled to begin a major initiative on a Wednesday morning. He came to us on Tuesday to tell us that his brother had just had a major heart attack. "I'll be here to get this going," he said. "I may be a little distracted, but I want you to know that I'll be there."

We told him to go home. "But how can I do that?" he asked. "Who will conduct the training program?" We told him that we would handle it. Family comes first, we explained, and we stepped in to handle his duties so he could be with his brother.

After that, we knew we could always count on him. He knew we cared about him, and therefore he cared about us. From that day on, if we ever needed someone to step up to the plate, to take on additional responsibilities, or to simply stay late to help out, he was the first one to volunteer. That gesture of kindness and sacrifice cemented our relationship—and we have found that it is a style of leadership that pays off in many ways.

Employees want leaders who care about them, who show compassion, but who also hold high standards for behavior, performance, and attitudes. Such leaders will reach out to people, seeing something in them that others might not. They allow room for mistakes and risk taking. They provide the support and resources necessary for success. They function as a coach, offering the guidance and feedback that builds people up.

Taking care of your employees is not only about salary, retirement plans, and medical benefits. It is about inviting them to share their thoughts and ideas and to take risks through innovative thinking. They will do so only when they feel safe and cared for. This is truly the greatest gift that leaders can give to their employees.

BRINGING OUT THE BEST

Traditionally, when business leaders talk about "supervision," they are referring to the managerial or leadership function of overseeing the productivity and progress of employees who report directly to the supervisor. Our approach takes a very different perspective. We define supervision more from a coaching and mentoring perspective than from a managerial perspective. Our approach is one of servant leadership.

Traditional managers are concerned, first and foremost, about productivity. The emphasis is on following rules, timelines, and everything going according to plan. They strive to make sure that everyone is moving forward to accomplish a goal. By contrast, coaching and mentoring emphasize personal growth to bring out the best in the employee. Instead of just enforcing rules and regulations and quotas, the coach/mentor will challenge the employees to improve their game and stretch to the next level.

Effective supervisors strive to unite their team. They build a culture of care and concern throughout the organization. They must be more than content experts. They must embrace the role of coach, creating a safe environment in which employees can work through developmental issues and concerns and grow both personally and professionally.

Unfortunately, many leaders today still do not understand that to inspire and motivate people, they must do more than just issue orders and give them a paycheck. No longer will employees be grateful just to have a job and tolerate being underappreciated or ignored. In today's prevailing culture, employees expect acknowledgment, and they expect it promptly. The paycheck alone isn't enough. They feel they have a right to a greater reward, and they won't be willing to knuckle under to an authoritarian supervisor. Instead, they want a supervisor who isn't bossy, who cares about them personally, and who is interested in nurturing their growth.

It is often suggested that today's younger generations have a culture of entitlement and insist on immediate gratification—a reflection, perhaps, of the immediacy of the technology age. Those traits generally are portrayed negatively, but there is a positive side as well: today's employees feel entitled to be treated well, and they don't want to wait for it. They are more demanding than ever about what they expect to get out of a job. If they feel dissatisfied or unappreciated, employees today often will quit a job without having another one lined up—something their elders would never have considered. They want to grow, and if they don't feel that they are advancing their careers, they will move on.

If organizations are to retain talent, then business leaders must wake up to that trend. Their approach to leadership must nurture people rather than merely drive them. As many organizations have come to recognize that need, we have been seeing a new age of leadership emerging that focuses on caring for and serving others.

LEADING FROM THE HEART

Understanding the need to nurture employees is just the start. Supervisors must put the servant leadership style into practice. They can adopt effective communication and listening skills, for example, and they can put in place techniques of conflict resolution and crisis management. Those will certainly help to improve the workplace climate.

At the core, however, what must change is that we must lead with our hearts. True strength, power, and control arise from a willingness to share vulnerabilities. When leaders let others see their humanity—including their weaknesses—relationships will blossom.

We are not suggesting that as a servant leader, you must bare your soul to your employees. We are saying that honesty and openness are crucial to developing meaningful bonds. When you show your employees that you are human, when you can admit your mistakes, they in turn will be more open and honest with you. Leading from your heart, rather than from a prescribed set of rules and regulations, will build a powerful sense of loyalty and commitment among your employees.

Those are the qualities that you want to encourage, and you can do so by developing a true human connection. The ability to share vulnerabilities builds empathy and compassion. Demanding perfection seldom produces the desired results. If a supervisor is perfect, then perhaps he or she has a right to demand perfection. However, we have yet to meet one who is.

Supervisors who concede that they are capable of making mistakes, by contrast, signal to their employees that they accept them and will accept missteps on their path to growth. That is not a prescription for poor performance. That is allowing them the freedom to take the risks that ultimately bring the best results. Otherwise, you squelch the spirit of innovation that prevails at the most successful enterprises. You are hurting the bottom line that you think you are protecting.

The attitude of "my way or the highway" tells people that you really don't care about them or their ideas—that they are cogs in your wheel. It is a dehumanizing way to treat people. If you want employees to develop loyal bonds with you so that they feel motivated to do their utmost, then you should show them your heart. You need not wear it on your sleeve, but it is important that they know you have one. Then you can move forward not in an atmosphere of fear but rather in one of respect and trust.

A TRULY OPEN-DOOR POLICY

To unite your team, you need to build relationships. As a supervisor, you must work to develop goodwill between yourself and the team, as a whole, and with each individual on it. You must also encourage the members of your team to understand and get along with one another. The quality of those relationships will have much to do with how effective your team can be in accomplishing whatever mission is set before it.

This will require more than pretty words. You must do more than just declare that you have an "open-door" policy. You need to make it happen. You need to make yourself available. Get up and move around. Circulate among your employees. Interact with them. You have a responsibility to take the initiative to talk to your people and to engage with them. If you truly see the value of an open-door policy, then what you do will be far more meaningful than what you say.

For many supervisors, an open-door policy amounts to this: "Look, I'm here—so if you want to talk, you know where to find me." That's not good enough. For a variety of reasons, some employees will feel uncomfortable or unsafe approaching you that way. You need to take the initiative and seek them out.

One helpful strategy is to schedule regular one-on-one meetings with each employee. We have found that many supervisors don't do that. They only talk to their employees when they have a problem with something or somebody or when an individual comes to them with an issue or a complaint. We suggest that supervisors meet with each employee weekly, biweekly, or at least monthly. This is an opportunity to ask questions such as: *What am I doing that you like or don't like? What can I do more of or less of? What can I stop doing or start doing? How can I better serve you as a supervisor?*

That last question is the crux of the matter. By meeting regularly with each employee, you can gather valuable feedback on how you can best serve your people. At the same time, you are clearly communicating to one and all that you believe their success is the measure of your own success.

You can learn a lot from such interaction. You can learn how your style of leadership is affecting the employees—if they feel safe to tell you about it. You might hear comments such as: "I'd like you to give me a little bit more time to try to work things out before you jump in to solve it" or "I need more direction from you. You give me tasks to do, but you don't give me the boundaries, and so when I come back to you with something, you reject it because it's not what you wanted. If you know what you want, tell me."

Those are the sort of responses that supervisors often hear. Employees want clear direction, but they do not want to be micromanaged. They want to know that you are there to support them and that you are following up on what they are doing, but they want the freedom to tackle the task using their own ingenuity. They want to be trusted. They want the satisfaction and dignity of figuring it out for themselves, and if they want help, they will ask for it. Within reason, supervisors should encourage that desire. It's how people grow.

As you get to know your employees, you will learn about more than their work. As those relationships grow, they will fill you in on their personal life as well. In your one-on-one meetings, ask them questions about their family, their vacations, and how their children's ball games have been going. You will be showing not only that you are listening to them but that you also care about them as people.

BUILDING HEALTHY RELATIONSHIPS

Getting to know people, after all, is the only way that you can expect to build relationships, which develop over time through personal interaction and the sharing of experiences and interests. Relationships grow as people live life together. They grow as people recognize how they are compatible in their behaviors and values.

As a supervisor, you will discourage healthy relationships with employees if you criticize them publicly or behind their back, if you allow no room for risk taking or mistakes, if you "hover" over them so that they feel little sense of privacy, if you fail to set clear expectations and to consistently enforce them, or if you assume you know how they are feeling and what they are thinking.

Developing relationships with your employees does not mean that you should try to be their peer. If you are a parent, then you probably understand that your role is not to be your child's best friend. Your role is to be the caring parent, not the confidant. That's not to say that supervisors should treat employees as if they were children, but the comparison helps to illustrate this point: employees need and want their supervisor to act as a supervisor, not just as another face among their ranks.

When we coach supervisors, we tell them that it's okay to become friendly with their employees, but they should be extremely cautious in hiring their friends as employees. It must always be clear who is in charge and who reports to whom. You might socialize together or go fishing together, but never forget that on the job it will be only one of you, when push comes to shove, who will make the final decisions. If you become too chummy with your employees as a group, then you likely will find that some of them will start taking advantage of you. Be careful. Friendships are good, and they will develop—but you must not try to be everyone's friend. Your employees must perceive you as the leader who will be fair and impartial. They need to understand that leadership is not based on the buddy system.

To unite the team, you must work on building healthy relationships not just *between* you and your employees but *among* the employees. Cultivating those relationships is one of the most important yet challenging goals for today's leaders. The success of your organization depends on whether you can create a culture of cooperation and collaboration. You need to get along well with your employees, they need to get along well with you, and they need to get along well with one another.

The power of those relationships is what will propel your team to excellence. Supervisors who encourage positive relationships find that they spread and grow rapidly. The spirit of goodwill is contagious. Ultimately, the benefit extends to the customers or clients or whomever the organization serves.

DEFINING AND DEVELOPING A CULTURE

What are some things that you can do to develop a culture of strong employee relationships? One goal is to make sure that everyone understands and buys in to a shared mission and vision. That means more than just being on the same page. It means your employees should help to write that page. The leadership needs to establish a clear mission and vision, but the employees should be able to contribute within those parameters.

We suggest that you develop a "culture statement" that includes your organization's mission, vision, and shared values. As much as the leadership feels is appropriate, the employees should be involved in helping to create and review that statement. That way, it is not just some edict from on high that hangs on the wall, seldom read or noticed. Instead of rolling their eyes, the employees feel a sense of ownership and pride in what it says. After all, these are "shared" values. The statement is not just something issued by the managers. It is a product of the community, and everyone takes it to heart because it reflects the values of all their hearts.

Once it is drafted, the culture statement can be put to good use in recruitment and hiring. To anyone who considers joining the team, the statement will serve as a clear notice of what the organization is all about. Anyone who signs on to work there, in other words, will be expected to commit to those values and embrace them in all they do. The culture statement also should be front and center during performance appraisals. The employees, during coaching, can consider whether what they are doing is getting them and the organization closer to the stated mission, vision, and values. Supervisors can thereby use the statement to help keep everyone on track with what they all have agreed is important.

The Walt Disney Company is exemplary in how it ensures that its mission, vision, and shared values permeate the organization. Disney emphasizes to its employees the importance of its four "keys" to excellent service: safety, courtesy, show, and efficiency. Each of the "cast members" is expected to put safety first, to be courteous and respectful to all guests, to be "show-ready" and stay in character, and to use time and resources wisely. All new hires know they must abide by these governing values.[3]

Diversity is another essential element of a strong workplace culture. This is not just a matter of racial and ethnic diversity. The organization must accommodate people's individual styles. Some are emotional and expressive, and others are analytical and practical. It is the nature of some employees to focus on people and their concerns, while others will focus on productivity and getting the job done. Every employee has a strength to offer, and when an organization builds on all those strengths, it becomes greater than the sum of the parts. Great leaders will look to hire people who can do things that others cannot. If everyone thinks the same way, stagnation will set in. A strong organization draws on a diversity of backgrounds, experiences, and mind-sets. Variety is the spice.

If a strong culture is to develop, the workplace must be a safe environment for dialogue and discussion. Employees should feel free to challenge and question and voice an opinion without fear of being fired. An environment like that must be encouraged from the top down. The leadership should emphasize that the culture will accommodate all points of view. Once the employees feel confident that they can speak their minds without retribution, then the organization will benefit from the free flow of ideas.

---

3   J. Jeff Kober, *The Wonderful World of Customer Service at Disney* (Performance Journeys, 2009).

The organization also will benefit when employees feel that their life outside the workplace matters to their supervisors. In some workplaces, employees are expected to be all business. No personal pictures are allowed in the work area, for example, and personal emails are forbidden. The rationale might be to keep family issues from encroaching on job duties, but the message that the employees get is that the leadership is indifferent or uncaring about their personal life. Offering them reasonable flexibility in their work schedules is one way to acknowledge their need for balance.

The workplace culture will grow dynamically when you create opportunities to share personal and family accomplishments. As you go about your day, touch base with your people and take a moment to chat about what is important to them at home. Make sure that you start out those regular one-on-one meetings with a few minutes of the human touch: *So how did your daughter's big softball game turn out? Has your son decided which college offer he'll accept?* Some supervisors are personable by nature, but others need to develop and practice the art of the "small talk" that can yield such big improvements in relationships and productivity.

The opportunities for interaction are many. Supervisors can set up summer barbecues and family health and fitness programs, for example, and other activities that bring employees and their families together. In a healthy culture, people will be having fun. It will be clear that they enjoy being with one another.

When we visit workplaces, we listen for the laughter. What is its nature? Does it continue when the supervisor enters the room, or does everybody shut up? Are the employees laughing at the manager or with the manager? Are they mocking the latest initiative or celebrating their mutual accomplishments? The laughter is a litmus test of the quality of the workplace relationships. When an atmosphere of fun prevails, that doesn't mean less work is getting done. It means you have a vibrant culture in which everyone is in the mood to stick around and do whatever it takes to build for success.

Here are some things you can do to unite your team:

- Maintain an open-door policy.
- Hold regular one-on-one supervisory meetings.
- Hold regular team meetings.
- Work side-by-side with employees.
- Lead by example.
- Create opportunities to share personal and family accomplishments.
- Provide flexibility in work schedules.
- Deal with conflict honestly and openly.
- Find out what motivates individual employees.
- Have *fun*!

Applying the principles:

- Select an employee with whom you want a better relationship.
- Determine at least two strategies to build that relationship.
- Implement those strategies.

"Outstanding leaders go out of their way to boost the self-esteem of their personnel. If people believe in themselves, it's amazing what they can accomplish."

— SAM WALTON

CHAPTER 3

PRAISING OTHERS

As the camp counselors got to know Coach as both a friend and mentor, it became clear that he was good at offering continuous praise and encouragement. He made an art of it. Here is just one example of how Coach built his team that way.

One day, as several counselors were chatting outside headquarters, Coach came by and joined the conversation. During a lull in the talk, he turned to one of the lifeguards and said, "Alex, I want to thank you for what you did at the ball field this morning. I noticed you talking to one of the younger boys who was crying. When you found out he'd hurt himself, you personally walked him to the infirmary—even though you were off duty and he wasn't assigned to your bunk. Great job! Thanks for caring so much about all the kids."

As a result of that interaction, not only did Alex know exactly what he had done right and that Coach appreciated it but the other counselors also knew what was expected of them in similar situations—and what it would take to get that kind of praise from Coach.

As the old saying goes: "You can catch more flies with honey than you can with vinegar." In other words, you will get far more from your employees by catching them doing what's right rather than catching them doing what's wrong. If you want them to behave or act in a certain manner, praise and encouragement will build morale and engagement. Criticism damages both.

To be effective, however, your words must be genuine and timely. You must do more than offer general statements of appreciation and dispense a few pats on the back. The praise must point to examples. Otherwise, you might as well save your breath. Your employees will perceive your words as shallow and contrived. Having heard it all before, they will recognize the insincerity and question your motives.

Praise must be accompanied by encouragement if it is to be effective. You encourage when you are specific about what you have observed and tell your employees to keep up the good work. It's a form of on-the-spot training. You are pointing out what is admirable about their efforts, and you are doing so publicly. Employees thrive on such recognition, and they will do what it takes to get it.

Let's say you notice Cindy taking a call from an upset customer. "Yes, sir," you hear her say, "I understand it's frustrating that you haven't received your shipment, and we're going to get to the bottom of this right now and find out why." She proceeds to resolve the issue courteously and professionally. As her supervisor, you take a moment to tell Cindy publicly what you observed. You are communicating more than just your satisfaction with her performance. You are also reinforcing the standard that you expect of her and her colleagues. Not only would you make Cindy's day but she likely would tell others about your kind words. They would see what they, too, must do to get such praise.

When you encourage one, you encourage all. You are signaling to all your employees that you are alert and paying attention. If they know that you see them doing those good things, then they will also realize that you will be seeing them if they make a mistake. You are demonstrating your vigilance by communicating, in a nice way, "Keep on your toes, folks, because I care and am aware of how we are all doing." You make that point well through your examples that compliment rather than reprimand. You build morale rather than diminish it. Your employees will respect you for it. Nobody wants a supervisor who is clueless.

Just be careful that your praise doesn't descend into platitudes. That is why you must be specific in your examples. If you just say, "Great job, way to go," the employee might be left wondering whether you even know what that job is. Much better to say: "I appreciate the care you took in writing that proposal, Juan. It's going to get us a big contract." That's specific to the employee, to the job, and to the task. And it doesn't mean that you won't be holding Juan accountable if he fails to live up to expectations. You should make it clear to the staff that although the emphasis will not be on reprimands, there are times when they are appropriate.

HOW TO DELIVER PRAISE

To develop a healthy organizational culture, your positive statements to the staff should far outweigh your negative ones. Scholars have gone so far as to come up with a 5:1 ratio, but the point is, even though you will need to clearly identify mistakes and problems, you can always do so while emphasizing the successes.

"To effectively motivate and retain employees," says Marcus Buckingham, author of *First, Break All the Rules*, "a manager needs to deal with each person one at a time—asking questions of, listening to, and working together one-on-one."

How do you initiate such conversations? Try some of the following openers. We can just about guarantee that the employee will want to hear more:

- "Thanks, you really made a difference when you . . ."

- "You are really doing top-quality work on . . ."

- "We couldn't have done it without your . . ."

- "One of the greatest things I enjoy most about you is . . ."

- "I'm really impressed with . . ."

The rest of what you say will depend, of course, on the nature of your organization and the tasks at hand. In general, however, there are several things to consider so that your words will be most effective. Here are some tips to observe when offering praise and encouragement:

- Be spontaneous. Catch your employees in the act and thank them right then and there. Don't wait for a staff meeting or luncheon. Be encouraging on the spot.

- Be specific. Provide concrete examples of what you like.

- Be purposeful. Go out of your way to show appreciation as a structured part of your daily routine. Consider it part of your job description to offer praise and encouragement. Get up, get out of your office, and find that praiseworthy person.

- Offer praise privately. Tell the employee in person what you observed. He or she will see it as an expression of personal appreciation.

- Offer praise publicly. Let the staff know what you have observed. This is the time to talk about it at the staff meeting or luncheon—after you have thanked the employee personally.

- Offer praise in writing. Send a thank-you note personally. Don't have your secretary do it for you. And handwrite it. Remember, you want to be genuine and authentic. A text message doesn't feel as soulful as paper and ink.

WHAT TRULY MOTIVATES?

If you ask ten supervisors what they believe motivates their employees, you might get ten different answers. Some of those answers will be spot on, some will be questionable, and others will be based on common myths. Much has been written about motivation in the world of academia; there is a chapter on motivation theory in virtually every management book ever written. You don't need to be a professor, though, to know intuitively what works—and it helps to know what doesn't work. Understanding what motivates people simply requires a knowledge of human nature.

People like to think they can motivate others, but *motivation must arise from within.* The best you can do for others is to create opportunities so that they can choose for themselves what will fire them up. Think of it this way. A teacher doesn't teach. A teacher lays out a smorgasbord of information from which students, if they choose, can fill their plates. They choose what they want to learn. Just as people have differing tastes for food or for education, they also will be different in what motivates them.

Money is not necessarily a good motivator. It's not typically for love of money that employees head elsewhere. It's because they don't love their jobs. Research shows that it takes a much greater salary increase to lure employees away from jobs they enjoy. Some supervisors believe that fear is a good motivator. They behave like frustrated parents yelling at the kids or like a blustering drill sergeant. Sure, the authoritarian style will produce immediate action and compliance, which we need on the battlefield—but do we want to treat our employees that way? If you browbeat your employees into submission, will they still obey you when you are not around? That will happen only if they have decided for themselves that you are right.

As a supervisor, you certainly can do a lot to motivate your employees. This is not something complex that should be left to the human resources department. Learning how to motivate can be as simple as asking employees a few questions: *What makes you feel excited about coming to work? What makes you want to do your best?*

And when you do ask such questions, expect a variety of answers. You are dealing with people from diverse backgrounds. Traditionally, retirees were given a gold watch. Today, many companies hand their employees a catalog from which to choose gifts on their service anniversaries. When we worked together, we found that many employees actually chose a chainsaw as their gift for twenty years on the job. Why? A lot of them lived out in the country, and for them the chainsaw was the most appealing thing in the catalog.

The question for supervisors, then, is this: What is the best thing that you can offer in your "catalog"? Some folks will want the gold watch, and some will want the chainsaw—but what will all of them find useful? We have found that praise, presented authentically and generously, will appeal to your employees' natural inclinations to accept responsibility and showcase their talents. When your people are working at their top level, so is your organization—and that is what supervising is all about. It's not about micromanaging and controlling and correcting. It's about encouraging and developing. That is your job.

Here are some things you can do to praise and encourage others:

- Celebrate with an awards banquet or other formal recognition.

- Compliment informally by catching employees doing the right things.

- Encourage staff members to recognize other staff members.

- Acknowledge efforts as well as achievements.

- Be sincere and specific in your praise.

- Publicly acknowledge good work at staff meetings.

- Offer recognition and rewards.

- Post your letters of appreciation on the bulletin board.

Applying the principles:

- Select appropriate employees.

- Find out what really motivates them.

- Praise at least three employees in the coming week, using this chapter's tips.

"Greatness is not a function of circumstance. Greatness, it turns out, is largely a matter of conscious choice and discipline."

— JIM COLLINS

CHAPTER 4

EXPECTING EXCELLENCE

Coach was one of a kind at setting high standards. He was always clear about what he expected, whether for small daily tasks or for the summer's performance goals at the camp. You never had to guess where you stood with Coach or what he wanted.

The counselors loved to tease Coach about being a stickler when it came to the proper way to pack a cubby. Each summer, he would train the counselors on how to teach the kids to pack a neat cubby and keep it clean. He would demonstrate how to fold clothes, point out the proper shelves for them, and stack shoes. He led by example.

One morning, a week before the visiting day for parents, the owner of the camp met with all the group leaders and counselors to insist that we spruce up the grounds, make the bunks look their best, and be on our best behavior. One counselor rather arrogantly told him that would be hypocrisy and the parents should see the camp as it was. The owner was speechless. Coach jumped in to defuse the situation. He firmly but gently explained to the counselors that cleaning up the camp was like cleaning up your house when you expect visitors: "Wouldn't you do everything you could to make your house clean and nice for your company?"

His comment put it all in perspective. Coach was teaching the counselors about the importance of having high standards for both themselves and others. He taught them to be clear about what they expected and how it should be done and to support others when they ask for help.

According to an old story, an aide to former Secretary of State Henry Kissinger had been working for days on a report. He finally completed it and presented it to the veteran diplomat, who returned it with the comment, "Is this the best you can do?" The aide, eager to please, spent several days revising it, but Kissinger returned it again with the same comment. After a third try, and getting the same response, the aide tossed the report down on Kissinger's desk and said, "Yes! Yes! This *is* the best I can do!" To which Kissinger responded: "Good! Then this time I'll read it."

You might call that an illustration of the expectation of excellence. Or you might call it something else, but it's a story that has long made us smile.

The pursuit of excellence is the ultimate objective of servant leadership. A major misconception about servant leaders is that they are soft and without purpose or direction. Nothing could be further from the truth. It is true that servant leaders strive to treat people with the dignity and respect they deserve, if you want to call that soft, but they also are hard on the issues and stand firm in their resolve. In the workplace, they set high standards for employees. They expect excellence.

Many organizations today suffer from failure to set high expectations. It seems as if leaders are afraid to challenge their employees. Some of that fear may come from the fact that we have become a very litigious society. It seems that whenever people are unhappy about something, they file a lawsuit. Supervisors also hesitate to demand more from their employees because it's so hard to replace them if they get upset and leave. With our changing technology, the world has become a smaller place. You can find a job almost anywhere and anytime. It seems that employees who are unhappy, for any reason, are willing to quit and move on, figuring they will land another job soon.

The good news is that both employer and employee, at the core, are in search of excellence. The employee wants an excellent job, and that does not mean one where supervision is lax and expectations are low. When people move on, it often is because they feel they are stagnating rather than growing and improving. Their desire to make the most of themselves is in line with the employer's desire for top-notch performance.

Assume the best of your people. Proceed from the presumption that they are striving to do excellent work, not that they don't care or that they are trying to undercut you and the organization. If for some reason they should prove you wrong, then you might offer more intensive training—and if that doesn't work, help them transition elsewhere. Just don't adopt the mind-set that people by nature are screw-ups. You should expect "the best you can do" the first time and every time.

EXCELLENCE FROM DAY ONE

You can begin to demonstrate your expectation of excellence by the way you recruit and hire the right employees. Do you let prospective employees know what they will be required to achieve if they work for you? Is it clear in your advertisements and in your recruitment efforts? Do you emphasize those standards during the interviews?

You should set high expectations not only for the job description and responsibilities but also for how employees will perform their duties. In other words, let people know that you will require them not just to accomplish their job duties well but that they must also do so with the right attitude. Let them know that you will not tolerate them on your staff if they wreck relationships. Even if they do superb work, they must also demonstrate that they can get along with people. A high-performing workforce requires nothing less, and you should insist on it.

The standards that you set should apply not just to the individual but to the entire staff. Consistency is essential. You are communicating not just how one person will behave but also the attitudes that the greater organization embraces. Some organizations, particularly larger ones, issue a policy manual to help explain procedures and expectations. If it is clear and concise, a policy manual can be useful.

Newly hired employees should go through a comprehensive orientation. This is the time to instill in them a thorough understanding of your organization's mission, vision, values, and goals. Well before they begin work, they should get a clear written description of what the position entails. Very often, those job descriptions are written in such general and vague terms that the expectations are up to interpretation. How do you hold an employee accountable if you haven't made it clear what the job requires? "So, how do you like your new job?" you may have asked someone, only to hear in response that he or she isn't sure yet what the job is. When we hear that, we know that the organization didn't provide a clear position description.

During the "honeymoon period," as the employee becomes more comfortable and competent, you should schedule regular feedback sessions with the employee to provide both training and encouragement. As this person's supervisor, you will want to touch base personally and regularly. Clarify how you perceive the goals and expectations of the position. Come to an agreement with the employee on the definition of excellence as it applies to the job. It helps to provide some models and specific examples of what that excellence looks like, even with the little things.

TAKING THE HIGH ROAD

When you set a high standard for others, you need to meet that standard as well, day in and day out—and that can be inconvenient. A big reason that some supervisors might be afraid to set high expectations is that they don't want to be held to those same standards.

Let's say you were considering a policy that everybody must show up at 8 a.m., no exceptions. And that, of course, would include you. If you didn't hold yourself to that standard, how could you expect others to take you seriously if you tried to hold them to it? You might feel tempted to overlook others slipping in at 8:30 so you could show up late at times, too. The consequence, however, easily could be that the culture eventually would shift to one of "come and go as you wish."

As a supervisor, you must model the behavior that you expect. If you don't want your employees to bring their kids to work, then you must never bring your own kids to work. If you expect your colleagues to share a room when traveling on business, then do the same when you are traveling. If you ask your secretary to run personal errands for you, then don't be surprised if others use their secretaries that way, too.

In other words, if you are going to set high expectations, then you must be willing to meet them yourself. First, however, you must communicate precisely what you expect. You cannot assume that employees will know what you want them to do and how well you want them to do it. Tell them. And follow through. The more clearly you can set expectations and goals up front, the less time you will waste later having to clarify what you meant—or worse, arguing about it.

Nobody wants to be the bad guy. That's why so many parents fail to hold their children to high expectations. They anticipate resistance and even confrontation, and so they do not take the constructive approach. Clarity at the start could prevent many an argument. The message within families and organizations should be this: *This is how we do business here, and we do it by building people up, not tearing them down.*

Supervisors must take the high road. For example, how do you respond the first time somebody is late for work? Do you go on a rant? Or do you say something like this: "Jane, I noticed you were late this morning. Is everything okay?" If you start out blustering, you will feel like a tyrant if she tells you her mother had a stroke. All you need is some information. If she says her alarm didn't go off, you can respond kindly, "I certainly understand that. It's happened to me. But our expectation is that everybody will be on time."

You will notice that in such an exchange, you first should make sure the employee is all right. Show that you care foremost about the employee's well-being. Then, if possible, you can empathize—but nonetheless you highlight what is expected of everyone. Don't wait until the tenth violation, when the employee may wonder why you didn't seem to care all those other times. Supervisors sometimes hold off because the situation doesn't seem to be worth risking a confrontation. Unfortunately, it is the failure to be straightforward that increases the risk.

As we coach our clients, we spend a lot of time teaching them how to deal with employees in these positive, healthy ways that emphasize what they are doing right but that do not sidestep what they are doing wrong. In the quest for excellence, that is the essence of what it takes for success.

THE SMART-P APPROACH

To help ensure that you have set clear expectations, we recommend using the "SMART" criteria, a professional strategy often used in establishing goals and objectives and evaluating performance. We add to that acronym the letter P, like this:

- **S** imple: Is the objective presented in a way that is free of jargon and easy to understand?

- **M** easurable: Is there a way to assess the extent to which the objective has been achieved?

- **A** chievable: Is the objective possible? For example, jumping to the moon is a simple and measurable objective. It's not achievable, though.

- **R** elevant: Does the objective clearly relate to the job and the organization's needs?

- **T** ime-dependent: Is there a deadline, and is it being observed?

- **P** ositive motivation: Are the incentives to reach the objective in the form of a carrot or a stick?

Here are some things you can do in expecting excellence:

- Conduct thorough orientation for new employees.

- Provide clear job descriptions.

- Hold regular feedback sessions with the staff.

- Provide training on a regular schedule.

- Point to models of what excellence looks like.

- Agree on a definition for excellence.

- Set companywide standards, not just individual ones.

- Expect "the best you can do" the first time.

- Assume the best of employees in their pursuit of excellence.

- Lead by example.

Applying the principles:

- Select an employee.

- Identify an expectation that needs to be introduced or reiterated.

- Using the SMART-P criteria, work with the employee to write the specific expectation to be met.

"Executives owe it to the organization and to their fellow workers not to tolerate nonperforming individuals in important jobs."

— PETER DRUCKER

CHAPTER 5

REQUIRING ACCOUNTABILITY

Not only had he perfected the art of praise and encouragement but Coach was also a master at holding folks accountable when necessary and appropriate. You had to admire the man for his continuing support and follow-up.

One year, Coach asked one of the counselors to design a training program for the group on the appropriate use of discipline. After discussing all the details of the assignment, Coach looked at the counselor and asked, "What else do you need from me to be successful at putting together this program?"

Coach was subtly making three important statements about accountability and expectations. As a true servant leader, he was letting the counselor know that he was there to support him and to offer assistance if needed. He also was making it clear that he expected the counselor would indeed be successful at the task. Third, he was communicating that although he would be there for support, his expectation was that the counselor would be the one designing the program.

Coach's question was a brilliant one, and that counselor and the others would find themselves using it often throughout their careers, both to show support and to set high expectations. Many people don't know how to respond to the question at first—but over time, with trust and experience, they come to realize that the offer of support is genuine and that they will indeed be held accountable for the results.

Tony likes show tunes. In fact, he has been whistling and singing a lot of them since you hired him several months ago. He has also been making the rounds of the office to tell endless tales, crack stupid jokes, and otherwise distract and disturb his colleagues, including you, his supervisor. You have pointed this out to him several times, in a nice way: "Come on, Tony, let's get back to work now," or, "Hey, bud, how about holding it down?" Each time, he just seems to get more annoying. When he's not talking to others, he's jabbering to himself. His coworkers are complaining.

One day, after enduring yet another Groucho Marx impersonation, you have had all you can take. Tony has pressed your last button. You go to the human resources department. "We've got to do something about this guy," you say. "He's not working out here. He has to go."

"For just talking?" says the HR director.

"Well, he's been doing this since he got here. I've told him over and over again to cut it out."

"Okay, let's see your documentation," the HR director says.

"I was trying to be nice about it," you explain. "I didn't want to give him a warning or write him up until it was clear he just wasn't going to listen."

The HR director shrugs. "Then there's nothing much we can do here today," he says. "Let me know when you have something." He sends you on your way, and as you return to your office you hear, rising from Tony's cubicle, the shrill strains of, "The sun will come out tomorrow." You're thinking maybe it won't.

It's a classic case of failure to hold people accountable. Trying to be the nice guy, you let it get to this. Generally, accountability need not be disciplinary. To the contrary, it should be positive and educational in nature, and that is usually more effective than punishment. When you encounter a Tony, however, you need to have a formal system in place to enforce your organization's policies and values.

Employees have a responsibility to both do their job well and to serve the organization, following its rules and observing its values. It is the duty of their supervisors to uphold and reinforce that responsibility. They must require accountability.

CONSISTENT AND FAIR

One of the greatest challenges in holding people accountable is to do so consistently and fairly. You might think that those two qualities are the same thing, but they have very different implications for effective supervision.

Consistency is the quality of steady, predictable, reliable behavior. For example, as a supervisor you should be consistent between what you say and what you do—in other words, walk the talk. For example, never be late if you insist that others always be on time. If you are going to be a stickler about disheveled desks, first attend to your own mess. It's hard to get down on people about negative talk when a lot of it is coming from you. Be consistent with your directives and expectations and with how you hold the staff accountable.

Fairness, on the other hand, is the quality of being just or impartial. Fair does not mean equal. It does not mean that supervisors should mete out equal consequences, whether positive or negative, for employees' actions. In fact, to treat all the employees equally would be inherently unfair. Instead, the treatment should be based on the facts and the circumstances at hand.

Let's say Felix and Maria both are forty minutes late one day. Felix has been late several times previously, offering a variety of dubious excuses. Maria is the most punctual person on the staff, but today her bus broke down on the way into town so she walked the last ten blocks through a rainstorm. As a supervisor, you must be consistent. The policy is that employees must not be late, and so you address the situation promptly. You talk to both about what happened. That's where the consistency comes in. You put Felix on probation. You thank Maria for her diligence. Two tardy employees, two quite different consequences. You have been consistent in addressing your company's expectations—and nobody, except perhaps Felix, would doubt that the outcome was fair.

THREE TYPES OF ACCOUNTABILITY

Holding others accountable is one of the most difficult supervisory roles. It must not be some informal obligation to which you give a nod when delegating projects and assignments. It must be more than an afterthought. You need to build it into everything the team does. That requires prior agreement on expectations and an understanding of what will happen if those expectations are not met. Unless you have come to such an agreement, it will be extremely difficult to hold anyone accountable in a constructive way.

At Rising Sun Consultants, we find that most of our clients have experienced issues with accountability. We spend more time on that topic than probably anything else. We look at three types of accountability that all play a role in the success of an organization. They are personal accountability, peer accountability, and professional accountability.

Personal accountability ultimately is the most important. As a supervisor, it is your responsibility to encourage employees to hold themselves accountable and to reinforce their efforts to do so. They are showing themselves to be personally accountable when they are self-motivated to do what they need to do—and to do it well.

How do you encourage personal accountability? A good start is to instill in your employees a sense of independence, as we will explore in chapter 7. When you do so, you build a foundation of loyalty and commitment. When employees are engaged that way, the motivation they feel is not based on salary or rewards. It is based on an inner desire to do their very best. A good way to encourage that quality in others is by developing it in yourself. You can be the role model as you openly display your loyalty and commitment to your organization's values. Treat your employees well as you forge strong relationships. Do what you know is right. In short, hold yourself personally accountable for holding the employees accountable.

When your organization has strong *peer accountability* within a trusting team culture, all the staff members feel responsible for holding one another accountable. They don't run straight to the supervisor to address conflicts over performance issues, timeliness, or lack of cooperation and support. Instead, they are encouraged and trained to address such issues and concerns directly with the other employees involved.

Your duty as supervisor is to build trust in your team by ensuring that all the employees get the proper training to deal effectively with such matters. You will want to clearly establish the cultural expectations so that the employees are holding one another accountable in the right way to the right things. You can serve as coach and offer support, but whenever possible, the employees should resolve disputes among themselves in a constructive manner.

In addition to personal and peer accountability, your employees should feel a sense of *professional accountability*. In some instances, they have an obligation to their profession to do their best to uphold its standards. In all instances, they have an obligation to demonstrate professionalism in all their endeavors.

Professional employees do whatever it takes to reach the highest level of excellence in all they do. They demonstrate effective decision making in the choices they make on a daily basis. They treat others according to the values and standards set by the organization and they are committed to continuous learning and development. Your role as a professional supervisor is to provide the coaching, discipline, and support they need to be successful in whatever role they are assigned.

PROGRESSIVE DISCIPLINE

The purpose of holding employees accountable is to ensure that their behaviors and attitudes are consistent with the organization's values and standards. Though the goal is positive change, there will be occasions when they fall short of those standards and you will need to take disciplinary action.

In general, discipline should be progressive in nature—that is, each time you need to address a continuing problem, the consequences should become more severe and meaningful. That is not to say that the discipline might not be tough on the first offense: some behaviors cannot be tolerated. The first time you steal, for example, you're fired. The discipline must be appropriate for the behavior, and if it is egregious enough, then it's time to say goodbye. Generally, though, the consequences will get stiffer as the violations continue. The discipline may progress from a warning to a written reprimand to probation to suspension. Along the way, you could offer coaching and additional training. But sooner or later, unless the employee corrects the behavior, enough is enough.

In today's society, it is critical that you document all disciplinary actions so that you have a record of how you tried to resolve the matter. If you are like many supervisors, you may want to cut the employee a break the first few times. What that tends to do, though, is send the message, as it did with Tony, that the negative behaviors are acceptable. You can get increasingly frustrated, to the point of wanting to fire the offender—but if you haven't dealt with the infractions progressively, then you have no documentation of anything inappropriate. That is why it is essential to deal with the inappropriate behavior from the time it begins, keeping accurate and thorough records. In fact, you should keep such records for each of your employees, documenting the positive as well as the negative.

What constitutes documentation? It might be a written reminder, or it might be your summary of a verbal reminder. It could be a formal written warning, an incident report, a disciplinary letter, or other record of disciplinary action. Generally, the HR department will want to see formal documentation that is in the employee's file.

TIME TO TAKE ACTION

As you address inappropriate behaviors and attitudes, you don't need to enter into a formal procedure from the first infraction, although you still must document anything of significance. Most supervisors, in their daily interactions, take an informal approach that generally will be quite effective in helping employees to meet the organization's expectations.

It's informal, but it's clear and straightforward. The negative behavior needs to stop right away. Explain why it is unacceptable or inappropriate. Tell the employee about the rationale for the positive behavior that is desired. Make sure the employee understands, and then make sure he or she complies.

That should be sufficient intervention to get things back on track—except when it isn't. That is when we recommend a more formal approach that we call ACTION. The letters of the acronym serve as reminders of what you can do in more serious cases in which the behavior itself is way out of line or has been recurring without correction. These are fundamentals by which you can resolve such issues:

- **A for "ask questions."** Don't jump to conclusions or make assumptions about what somebody has done or the reasons. You need to ask the basic, open-ended questions: *Who? What? Where? When? Why? How?* Assess the situation.

- **C for "consider options."** Evaluate how you could handle the situation. Could you provide additional skills training? Is discipline warranted? Would a development plan be of help? What would happen if nothing were done? As a supervisor, you need to understand the policies of your organization so that you know which options are available to you. For example, do you even have the authority to suspend or fire an employee?

- **T for "talk about concerns."** Share your thoughts and concerns with the employee. Make sure expectations are clear, and give the employee plenty of opportunity to ask questions. During the discussion, share specific examples that demonstrate the issue.

- **I for "investigate facts."** Once you have gathered the details, investigate what is real. To the extent that is warranted, substantiate those details. If necessary in a serious case, talk to witnesses and check computer logs and security video images. Verify the credibility of the information you get. Separate emotions from the facts so that your decision is as objective as possible. Find out whatever steps were taken in the past when there were similar patterns.

- **O for "outcomes."** Decide the consequences. Now that you know what has happened, what are you going to do about it? Perhaps the employee will just be required to finish or redo the task. You may decide they require more training, with greater oversight. In some cases, raises or bonuses might be withheld, as well as opportunities for advancement. In any case, the discipline should be progressive, tied to the severity of the problem and how many times it has happened.

- **N for "next steps."** Outline how you will follow up. Write a formal plan for how you will determine whether behavior, performance, or attitude have improved. Decide how long the corrective steps will be in place, and set up a schedule to check in on how much progress has been made. All the follow-up measures and assessments must be documented in writing.

SKIN IN THE GAME

Supervisors who engage the whole staff in setting goals find that the employees feel more confident that they can achieve them and perform at a higher level. They know up front just what they need to do, and they will know whether they have hit the mark. They are not muddling through the day in uncertainty, wondering what is expected of them. And because they themselves have contributed to setting the expectations, they will feel a sense of ownership. They will have more "skin in the game." These are their goals, not somebody else's. Under those conditions, they will feel more personal accountability.

As a supervisor, you can encourage that accountability by clarifying the givens and the non-negotiables up front. When appropriate you can establish the outcomes and expectations in writing. Involve the employees as much as possible, giving them the authority to accomplish those goals without micromanaging them. You can provide assistance and coaching and ensure they have the necessary resources and training but don't take over their assignments.

Throughout the project, and at its conclusion, you can offer the employees meaningful feedback on how they are doing in terms of core beliefs, guiding principles, and shared values. You can do so both informally, on a daily or weekly basis, as well as formally, preferably on a quarterly basis if possible. Be sure to emphasize positive reinforcement for good performance. Make it clear what it means to meet standards and to exceed standards—and also the consequences of failing to meet those standards. Your employees will appreciate your performance appraisal and accountability systems if they see them as progressive and helping them to do the job well.

WHEN IT'S TIME TO TERMINATE

If the failure to meet standards and expectations means that an employee's job could be in jeopardy, state so up front. Supervisors must face up to the responsibility to let employees go when necessary and appropriate. If you have done everything possible to help the employee succeed, it's okay to say, "You're fired." You must be decisive in all your actions, and sometimes the ultimate step in holding an employee accountable is termination.

As you make the decision on whether to fire an employee, ask yourself the following questions:

- Did we make the right hiring decision in the first place?

- Did this individual, before accepting the position, get a realistic view of what the job would entail and of our expectations and values as an organization?

- Did the employee get a thorough orientation to the organization, the department, and the specific job?

- Did we provide the proper tools, training, and other resources necessary for the employee's success?

- Did the employee regularly get clear, written goals and expectations?

- Did the employee get continuing feedback and coaching support?

- Is there a different position elsewhere in the organization where the employee would be a better fit and able to thrive?

Once you have answered those questions, take decisive action. Even if you conclude that it was you who failed and not the employee, it may still be appropriate and in everyone's best interest to let that person go. In any case, it is imperative that you learn from the situation and improve your commitment and support to all your employees.

Here are some things you can do in requiring accountability:

- Provide regular feedback.

- Respond immediately to inappropriate behaviors.

- Create a culture where employees hold themselves accountable.

- Create a culture where employees hold one another accountable.

- Adopt a performance appraisal system.

- Establish measurable goals for action steps.

- Follow through on accountability measures.

- Take action and learn from mistakes so they don't repeat.

- Once you decide on a change, stick with it.

- Include the staff in formulating workplace rules and values.

Applying the principles:

- Choose one concern about employee performance that you have dealt with in the past month.

- Evaluate how you used, or could have used, the ACTION process.

- Determine what you feel you did well and where you might have made different choices.

"Our mission and core values drive our culture and are the foundation of our practice. We measure each decision against these standards."

— CHRIS HANSLIK

CHAPTER 6

VALUING WHAT YOU BELIEVE

One of the critical lessons that Coach taught the camp counselors over the years was the importance of a shared set of values and beliefs—and he didn't mean in words only. He wanted to see consistency in their attitudes and behaviors.

At the beginning of every summer, Coach led the counselors in developing what he called a "behavioral agreement." He reviewed with them the camp's mission statement and the shared values and expectations. Coach explained that declarations like those would be meaningless without accountability. Unless the counselors adopted behaviors that they could observe and measure, those statements would just be nice words hanging on the wall. They would mean something different to everyone who read them.

Each year, the counselors came up with basically the same behavioral agreement. They defined and described their shared values and expectations in similar ways. Still, each new group of counselors felt committed to the agreement that they themselves had drafted. The counselors made strides in their willingness to hold themselves and, when appropriate, one another accountable for how they behaved.

When was the last time you read your organization's mission statement and reflected on each word? Have you paid much attention to the vision statement or the statement of shared values? Do you know what your organization stands for? Are you clear about your role in it?

Even if you have memorized each word and recite those statements daily over breakfast, how well do those you lead understand their roles and responsibilities and how they affect the mission and vision? How are you helping to advance that understanding? Do your employees contribute to other areas in the organization, and are you helping to ensure that collaboration across departments?

Those questions get to the core of what matters most in a healthy organization. Often, people get so busy with strategy, tasks, and technology that before long the vitality is gone, along with the best employees. They forget what it's all about.

Think about a good experience you have had with a restaurant or hotel. What made it memorable? It probably had a lot to do with the setting and how it appealed to your senses. You were treated courteously and professionally. The accommodations were clean and comfortable. No doubt the establishment had a clear vision for how the public would perceive it. It knew its values and stayed true to them.

The most successful organizations have built and maintained a powerful culture. And just what is that? Your organization's culture is reflected in the feeling you get when you wake up each morning and think about going to your workplace. It's in the thoughts that run through your mind after meetings. It's in the tone of those chats you have each day with employees. It's how you feel and what you observe when you walk through the doors to begin your day. It's in the way that you and your colleagues celebrate successes, strengths, and accomplishments.

Every organization has its own unique culture of shared visions, beliefs, and behaviors. The mission, if it means anything, is not just words on a poster. It is not a collection of dictates from the top managers announcing goals and directions and expecting everyone to get on board. The mission is a living, breathing declaration of what the organization represents and why it exists. That mission must be communicated clearly and widely; every employee must know his or her role in fulfilling the greater purpose.

In their pursuit of success, organizations must remember and cherish their founding principles. They must not lose sight of why they are here and what their people collectively were assembled to uphold and accomplish. In other words, they must value what they believe.

LIVING WHAT YOU BELIEVE

Effective supervisors support their employees in understanding their role and how it connects to the organization's mission, vision, and shared values. They need to see how they will impact the organization if they do their jobs well—and if they do not do them well. That is why we put so much emphasis on clear and thorough position descriptions. The behaviors that are expected of them on the job must be consistent with the values of the organization.

One of our clients is a Christian organization that strongly believes in the principle of turning the other cheek. Its mission statement emphasizes "Christ-like" behaviors, and by nature the leadership strives to give people second chances in the interest of "reconciliation." Although we ordinarily caution our clients not to be overly long-suffering with employees, this organization is demonstrating consistency with its stated values. It is linking those values to employee behavior. In this organization, people are living what they believe.

In chapter 2, we discussed how organizations can draft a culture statement to help unify the team. The culture statement also reflects and reinforces the shared values. In creating the culture statement, the organization can establish several clear behavioral examples for each of those values. On the list of those values are often words such as truth, integrity, and honesty. This is an opportunity to explain precisely what those mean. In doing so, those qualities become measurable. You can assess, for example, whether the organization and its people are exhibiting more honesty or less of it than they were previously.

Virtually every organization will list honesty as a core value. Asked what that means, most will describe it as telling the truth. Sounds good—but consider this statement: "You're looking rather fat today." It could well be the truth. It's also downright mean. Would you want to work with someone who would say such a thing? Honesty without tact is not always the best policy. That's just one example to illustrate why you need to take great care in defining those core values.

It's also why you should solicit the participation of your employees in drafting the culture statement. Your goal is to establish governing values that are specific and measurable. The top leadership may be establishing the overall direction, but it will be the employees who attend to how the specifics will be accomplished. Therefore, they should be involved in defining those specifics. They gain a sense of ownership in the process, and the organization gains a more diverse perspective. In working with our clients, we have found that we can assemble an employee group of any size and, within a few hours to a few days, reach a consensus on a culture statement—including mission, vision, and shared values. We call that the "discernment process," and it narrows the focus through deductive discussion.

That culture statement will serve as a guide for supervisors in dealing with employees whose issues go beyond their job duties. A big challenge for many organizations is what to do about employees who alienate themselves and others even though they do their job well. They get it done and may even do excellent work, but they have developed poor relationships with those around them because of their attitude and behaviors. Supervisors tend to feel more comfortable dealing with performance issues because they have the job descriptions and written expectations for what the employee is supposed to do. If the employee isn't doing the job, it's clear. But how do you respond to an employee's bad attitude or behavior? You might feel that it's a matter of opinion. It's subjective, and you might be uncomfortable saying anything. The culture statement helps to remove that uncertainty. It provides a clear directive on the attitudes and behaviors that will be acceptable.

Organizations that have established a clear direction and that define their values daily will find it easier to hire employees who are consistent with those values. If most of your people are on board with the mission and values, then not only will it be easier for them to succeed but it also will be harder for anyone to get away with poor performance, attitudes, and behaviors.

EVER GREATER HEIGHTS

As you can see, developing a strong culture involves far more than decorating the wall with declarations. When you are specific about the meaning of such words as integrity and honesty and why they matter, you will be giving the employees the gift of clarity and consistency. They will be better able to hold themselves and one another accountable to living out the beliefs that they have pledged to value individually and corporately.

It is a commitment to take quite seriously. Once an organization has drafted its culture statement, we encourage the leadership to have all employees sign a copy of the document to indicate their commitment to living by those values as part of their job responsibilities. A copy of that personal pledge should be included in each employee's file. Some organizations make the culture statement an integral part of each job description that employees sign when hired. In addition, a reminder of the values can be included at the top of all important documents, meeting agendas, etc. You may find it inspiring to start every meeting by asking for an example of how someone has exhibited one of those values. Keep them up front and center in all that you do.

We are talking here about the essence of servant leadership. We are talking about the sort of encouragement that leads people to ever greater heights. As a supervisor and leader in your organization, you must ask what you are doing to hold yourself and your employees accountable for supporting your shared values and pursuing your mutual mission.

That is why we have emphasized that those values should play a role in the hiring process and become part of each employee's position description. That is why you should highlight them during orientation programs and address them specifically and regularly in training and support sessions. During performance appraisals, do you talk about the greater vision as well as the specific tasks? It's one thing to go about meeting your numbers daily, but you also need to go about fulfilling your purpose daily.

The servant leader's job is to help others to see the big picture and to understand what's in it for them if they get on board. Effective supervisors regularly share organizational and departmental goals, values, and direction, both for the short term and the long term. They cannot convince others, however, unless they walk the talk. To get others to follow, you must demonstrate your commitment in words and actions. Otherwise, you lose credibility. Don't let that happen. Make sure that the one your employees want to follow is you.

Here are some things you can do to value what you believe:

- Define your culture intentionally so employees buy in to the mission and vision.

- Gain a consensus on a set of shared values and behaviors.

- Methodically plan how you will build and maintain your culture.

- Value diversity and understand differences in the workplace.

- Demonstrate compassion.

- Show respect by treating others as you would have them treat you.

- Conduct regular feedback sessions with staff.

- Offer feedback that ties people's decisions to the vision.

- Lead by example, living the shared values as a role model.

- Remind your team continuously of the goals and desired outcomes.

- Develop straightforward strategies to attain bold visions.

Applying the principles:

- Take note of a variety of the behaviors you see in your organization's culture.

- Make a list of the behaviors that reflect a positive culture.

- Make a list of the behaviors that reflect a negative culture.

- Decide on specific ways to implement a more positive culture.

*"You cannot help men permanently by doing for them
what they could and should do for themselves."*

—ABRAHAM LINCOLN

CHAPTER 7

INSTILLING INDEPENDENCE

Coach's mastery at delegation became abundantly clear one summer when he once again asked one of the more experienced camp counselors to take on the responsibility of developing and presenting a training program for the new counselors coming in.

As he worked with that young man, Coach demonstrated two of the most important rules of effective delegation: 1) Never "dump" a job on someone else; in other words, don't delegate something simply because you don't want to do it yourself or don't like the task; and 2) never "abdicate" your responsibility and assume that once you have delegated something, you are done with it.

Effective delegation requires the continued commitment and involvement of the delegator, who must offer that support without making the fatal mistake of micromanaging. Coach allowed the freedom to think and act independently while offering whatever guidance was appropriate.

The training program that the young counselor was asked to develop was on the use of incentives to motivate the campers. Coach did not just tell him to make it happen and walk away. Instead, he spent time with him to make sure that he would be successful.

The young man knew without a doubt that the program was his own to design and that he would be held accountable for its success or failure. However, it was equally clear to him that Coach was equally invested in his success. It was an example of how Coach pinned his own success to that of others. It was the type of collaborative or "win–win" approach that he taught those fortunate enough to have him as a mentor.

You have hired the people you felt were fit for the job. You felt confident that they possessed the talent and expertise to fulfill your organization's mission. You went in search of the brightest—and now that you have found them, it's time to let them shine.

If anyone ever has micromanaged you, you know how it feels—and it certainly was not an atmosphere of mutual respect. You could ask dozens of people whether they have experienced a work situation in which they were overly controlled. Most will say yes. Did they like it? They will say no.

If you truly hired your employees because you felt they were a good fit, then why would you cease to treat them that way on the job? Would they run off and cause trouble unless you kept them on a leash? Will they not produce unless you prod? If you felt they were capable, why not get out of the way and let them do the job? If you have concluded they cannot, then maybe this just isn't the place for them.

A powerful strategy of effective supervision is to allow employees to do their jobs without having to dictate the day-to-day specifics. Micromanagement strangles initiative. When you empower your people to do what you hired them to do, you develop an environment of hope, confidence, and autonomy. You believe in them, and you assume the best in them—and, therefore, you can instill independence.

DELEGATING THE DECISIONS

To encourage independence in the ranks of your workforce, you must allow your employees to make the appropriate decisions. Your organization has many things to do, and your staff possesses the spectrum of skills to make it all happen. You could not even hope to handle it all yourself. Without the support of others, you are incapable. You need to delegate responsibility and decision making to those whom you have hired to help your organization fulfill its mission.

Many supervisors struggle with effective delegation. It's a major challenge. Leaders may feel the need to attend to every detail for fear that others will be unable to do their job in the way they want it done. In doing so, it's the leadership that is falling short. If you hover over your employees, you essentially are saying that you do not value what they think, feel, and believe. You are saying that you consider them unworthy of what you hired them to do.

To delegate effectively is to allow autonomy. Strong leaders surround themselves with people whom they trust to make the appropriate decisions. Effective leaders understand that the folks they have hired have the expertise to accomplish what needs to be done and will take the right steps. Instead of micromanaging, supervisors must get out of the way. They should develop and support rather than control. They should foster independence. That is what we as citizens expect of our government, and that is what employees should expect of their leadership.

Independence does not mean isolation, however. The leadership must set the appropriate boundaries and remain involved, offering whatever support and guidance is necessary and appropriate for the situation. You are not sincerely promoting independence if you simply are dumping onto someone else a job that you want to get off your own plate.

Even when you delegate, the responsibility remains yours. You are allowing your trusted employees to do what they do best; your success depends on theirs. You must not abdicate that responsibility. You are handing over the task, but you are not washing your hands of it. You are stepping out of the way but not out of sight.

Just as you must draw clear lines on what you expect of the employees, so you must clarify the level of authority that you are granting them. If you are telling them that they can make their own decisions, what will be their level of authority? What is the extent of their autonomy? Is it absolute, or is it more advisory in nature? You can avoid a lot of frustration by defining in advance the nature of decision making in your organization.

Decision making comes down to four fundamental types:

1. *Majority rule.* This is the foundation of democracy. Reaching a decision requires the support or affirmation of at least 51 percent of the group members.

2. *Unanimity.* To reach a decision, all members of the group must agree. This is also common in democratic societies.

3. *Power of one.* The most powerful or influential person makes the decision, as in autocratic forms of government.

4. *Consensus.* After full discussion by all involved, the group comes to a majority decision and those who disagreed nonetheless support it.

An effective decision-making process, like most good systems, establishes boundaries for involvement. Everyone knows who can decide what and who reports to whom. Employees will know how and when they will be involved. The goal is to promote confidence and a spirit of collaboration. In healthy decision making, the leadership shares responsibility without losing control.

THE FIVE Cs OF DECISION MAKING

In most organizations, decisions will be made in some combination of decision-making model or strategy. One in particular which we have adapted from a model originally developed by Interaction Associates, LLC, is one we like to call the "Five Cs of Decision Making" and involves a combination of five basic decision-making styles: cloistered, cooperative, consensus, collaborative, and commissioned.

Let's look at each of those styles and the supervisory relationships that they describe.

In the *cloistered style*, the leader simply makes the decision and lets others know about it. The rationale is that it is efficient and swift. The leader has clear control and can make the decision without delay, seeking to minimize negative consequences. However, that leader may lack critical information, and others will not feel ownership of the decision because they did not participate in it.

In the *cooperative style,* the leader gathers feedback from several individuals or from the whole group and then makes the decision, sharing it with the group. By gathering opinions, the leader can make a more informed decision, which is particularly important when the outcome will affect all. The leader, however, does not relinquish the decision making to others. Group members who sacrificed their own ideas or desires may feel little sense of support.

In the *consensus style,* the group members brainstorm possible solutions and negotiate a decision, usually by vote, that everyone is willing to support and implement. Doing so helps to ensure that a variety of opinions are expressed and that everyone understands and is committed to the decision. This can take time, however, and the process is relatively complex. Group members who compromised— who agreed to disagree—may find it hard to support the decision.

In the *collaborative style,* group members challenge one another as they brainstorm in search of synergy in reaching a decision that everyone will support and be excited to implement. They are looking for the true "win–win." Because the entire team is engaged in seeking creative solutions, everyone feels ownership of the decision. Instead of agreeing to disagree, they work it all out. This style too, however, is time consuming and complex and may frustrate those who want quicker action.

In the *commissioned style,* the leader clearly establishes the parameters for a decision and then delegates it to an individual or group. The rationale here is to develop the highest level of member engagement and accountability. By entrusting the decision to others, the leader can focus on other important matters. Meanwhile, the team members feel a greater sense of responsibility and commitment to the success of the decision. Like some of the other styles, however, this is time consuming and complex—and the leader must accept the possibility that the decision will not represent his or her vision or direction.

Though most organizations will have a prevailing style of decision making, those styles tend to overlap and to play varying roles at varying times. For example, let's say you are a leader who is delegating, or commissioning, a task. You set clear parameters: "Paint this room any color except pink, turquoise, or puke green, and get it done by Friday with a budget of $1,000." The expectations and the degree of authority are clear. You agree to accept whatever the team decides to do within those parameters. If they want to go outside that box, they must come to you for permission.

The team members set to work, taking a collaborative approach. A day or two go by as they try to reach full agreement. The team supervisor sees that Friday is fast approaching and points out that one of the conditions under which the job was delegated was to get it done on time. "We need to settle for a consensus here," the supervisor says. "We need to get started on the painting today," she tells the group, "and if we can't reach that consensus now, I'm going to choose the color based on what I've heard you say so far. So just be clear: I'm ordering the paint at noon and telling the manager about our choice."

What is happening there is what Interaction Associates calls "fallback." As the leader, you commissioned the project to the painting team, which tried to collaborate but now must fall back to consensus, or potentially to the team supervisor's decision based on a cooperative approach. If that doesn't work, and the team fails to accomplish the job within your parameters, then you may need to resort to the cloistered approach if you ever want to see that room painted.

All that should be clear from the start. What upsets people is when the supervisor tells them they can collaborate but then steps in as if by whim to overrule them. "Why were we even asked," they may wonder, "if the decision was a foregone conclusion?" The process is much smoother when you clearly draw the boundaries for that collaboration and when everyone knows the next steps if that doesn't work out.

When the leadership is inconsistent in decision making, the employees feel frustrated. Imagine you called the staff members together and asked them what they wanted for lunch tomorrow. "I want chicken!" says Bill. "I'd like pizza!" says Judy. Having whet their appetites, you then serve them a platter of baloney. They quickly see that your questions served some purpose other than caring about what they truly wanted.

That is why we help our clients understand these models for decision making. Each of those five styles has a time and a place and a purpose. Each can be used effectively, and each can be used disastrously. If you only make cloistered decisions, your people may come to think of you as a dictator. If everything must be collaborative, you can seem indecisive, even incompetent.

As you advance toward the commissioned style of delegation, you increasingly are granting independence, but to some extent you could be sacrificing efficiency. Decisions likely will take longer, and time can be a precious commodity. On the battlefield, for example, the cloistered style saves lives—although delegation and trust also are essential to effective military leadership. Navy SEALs have autonomy that befits their training. They need not wait for every order.

In your organization, you must incorporate all those styles at the right times to the appropriate degree and find the best ways to involve your employees. You can make a cloistered decision to delegate, for example. When it is clear to the employees that you truly care what they think, then they will feel valued and motivated. You will be sincerely soliciting the full participation from your best and your brightest—and when you do, everyone wins.

Leadership is a learned behavior. Good supervisors are not necessarily born that way. They are open to discovering methods of decision making that enhance the independence and autonomy of their team. That's the way to build morale. That's the way to keep your employees engaged in both their own success and the success of your organization.

EMPOWERMENT THROUGH DELEGATION

When you effectively delegate responsibility, you empower your employees to reach their potential in ways that help your team and organization. As the leader, you are making a concerted decision to allow them that level of control over the work that they have been assigned. You are agreeing to accept what they do within the criteria that you give them. You are clear from the start about the results that you will accept, and you won't be altering those criteria once the employees have met them. If you do, you will kill morale.

If your organization is to thrive, your people must know that they can step out and try things. As the leader, you should encourage reasonable risk taking as an important part of instilling independence. Allow your employees to take some chances, knowing that it is okay to fail so long as they don't fail continuously at the same thing. If that is the case, then perhaps you need to clarify your expectations, improve accountability, or provide training and other means of support. Don't just say, "I told you so." Talk about what happened and why it didn't work. Ask them to look for another approach that might work better.

Remember that you are the coach. Your job is not to do the work for your employees. If that were the case, why would you need them in the first place? When you delegate effectively, not only are you instilling independence but you are also giving yourself the freedom to attend to the most important matters of your own position. As a servant leader, your role will be shifting from "managing" the productivity and progress of employees to mentoring them for their continued growth and development. In other words, your job is to lead. Your responsibility is to guide your "community" toward effective change.

To delegate well, not only must you be clear about the ground rules and expectations but you also must make sure that the resources are available to accomplish the task. You must regularly touch base to check on progress and be available for support, if requested.

You can delegate at differing levels, depending on the situation and requirements of the task—and the employee's level of comfort with autonomy. Here are some common variations on what you might communicate to the employee or the team:

- "Look into the situation, report back, and I'll decide what to do."

- "Look into the situation, report back, and together we will develop a plan."

- "Look into the situation, report back, and let me know what help you need from me in order to handle the situation."

- "Look into the situation, report back, and share both your analysis of the situation (reasons, options, pros, and cons) and your recommendation."

- "Look into the situation, decide, and then let me know your decision."

- "Look into the situation, decide, and take action. Let me know what you did (and what happened)."

- "Look into the situation, decide, and take action. No need to check back with me."

Each of those approaches can work well because each makes it clear what is expected. They each delegate responsibility to a greater or lesser degree, without doubt about how to proceed. As the leader, when you delegate tasks to people, they should be crystal clear when they walk out of your office about their role in the decision-making process.

Delegation is a matter of degree. It's not all or nothing. Simply asking someone to pull up a report for you is delegating. It's at a low level, but it begins to build trust and relationships. You start slowly, and as those relationships grow you eventually will identify employees who are best suited to join you in the leadership of the organization. You develop a culture of accountability, responsibility, confidence, and trust. Such is the power of delegation and instilling independence.

Here are some things you can do to instill independence:

- Learn to delegate appropriately.

- Encourage employees to take risks.

- Never micromanage.

- Encourage teamwork.

- Encourage independent decision making.

- Remember there is "no such thing as perfect."

- Provide a safe learning environment.

- Make sure all tasks are currently relevant.

- Lead by example: "show them, show them, show them."

- Authorize staff to "make it right" for customers.

Applying the principles:

- Choose a team member and decide on a task or project that you can delegate to that person.

- Determine the appropriate level of delegation and the nature of your continuing role after you assign the task.

- Set up and reach agreement on the ground rules, parameters, and expectations.

- Provide the necessary tools and resources.

- Monitor progress.

- Provide effective feedback.

"Research indicates that workers have three prime needs:
Interesting work, recognition for doing a good job, and being
let in on things that are going on in the company."

— ZIG ZIGLAR

CHAPTER 8

SHARING CONTINUOUSLY

No matter what the situation, Coach always kept the camp counselors as informed as possible. That didn't mean he told them every little detail of every situation; it meant that he always shared whatever information was necessary and appropriate. While Coach would be the first to agree that "information is power," he truly believed that power needed to be in the hands of those closest to the situation.

One summer, during the first week of camp, Coach shared with the counselors that one of the campers was very sick and might not make it through the season. It was heart-related and nothing contagious, he explained. Coach told the group that the young man had attended the camp every year for the past decade and that he and his parents had decided that he should try to spend one more summer there. Some of the counselors asked who he was, but Coach emphasized that the young man wanted to be treated no differently than the others and that the camp would maintain his dignity and confidentiality. Only his individual counselor and group leader would be informed of his identity and the details of his condition.

Halfway through the summer, the young man died of a massive heart attack. Because they had been informed of that possibility, the counselors were much better able to handle that awful news and focus their attention on helping the other campers deal with the loss of their friend. Coach had told the counselors just enough but not too much. He maintained a commitment to open and honest communication and trust as well as to the dignity of all involved.

Think back to a time when an important decision needed to be made in your workplace. What was your reaction? Did you make the decision on your own, or did you seek the advice of others who reported to you? If it was a group effort, was this typical in your decision-making process? If you felt that you alone needed to make the decision, how did you communicate that to the others?

If employees are to feel valued, communication must be open and honest and must flow both ways. Supervisors and employees must regularly share what is on their minds and in their hearts— and they must share continuously. Successful organizations don't just hope that will happen; they establish a system to ensure it will happen.

FOUR PARADIGMS OF COMMUNICATION

Over the years, we have employed four core paradigms of effective communication, combining our own ideas with some insights of others. We believe that it is virtually impossible to communicate effectively without observing these fundamentals:

Concern for others

- Demonstrate kindness, understanding, and care for others.

- Deal honestly and directly with the issues, while showing concern and respect.

Sense of humility

- "Pride is concerned with who is right. Humility is concerned with what is right." —Ezra Taft Benson

- Humility is not about tearing yourself down but about building others up.

Service above self

- Give back better than you are given.

- "People who succeed in leadership and life do not go around settling scores. They do not even keep score. They 'run up the score' by doing good to others, even when others do not deserve it." —Henry Cloud, from *9 Things a Leader Must Do*

Success

- Successful communication is defined by others, not by self.

- Successful communication is dependent upon everyone else's success. Both the sender and the receiver must understand the intent. You can say something repeatedly, but you have not communicated effectively unless the listener "gets it."

You will note that nothing in those paradigms requires that you must be highly articulate to be a good communicator. Instead, the emphasis is on reaching out to others and listening intently so that they feel valued. You should be striving for positive communication that is free of manipulation and contention. That is how you encourage employees to participate in the crucial exchange of ideas. The more that others see that you are genuinely committed to listening and the more they observe you responding appropriately, the more committed they will be to advancing the organizational goals and initiatives.

EFFECTIVE FEEDBACK

Proactive supervisors go out of their way to get feedback from their employees, recognizing that they are an important source of information about how to do a job and do it better. Instead of waiting for your employees to come to you with issues and complaints, you should go to them.

You need to create a safe and positive environment in which information flows freely and the employees can honestly express their feelings. Find a private place to talk, and ask for specific examples of how you might do better—and then listen attentively. Never become defensive. Thank the employee for the feedback, and be sure to follow up. Both of you will want to be sure that the message sent was the one received.

You also will need a private place to offer feedback to employees. An important element of that, as well, is to listen attentively to learn what you can before offering your thoughts. We teach a technique that we call the "question-based process." It's three simple steps. First, ask questions—probing, purposeful, and open-ended ones. Then, be silent and actively listen, making good eye contact and nodding to show you are paying close attention. Then respond by reflecting what you have heard, including the emotion that you perceived to be behind it.

Let's say it's time to talk to an employee about being late. The conversation might go like this:

"Jerry, I noticed this morning that you were kind of late," you say. "I'm curious what's happening. What's going on? Is there any way I can help you?"

"Stuff at home was kind of crazy. I'm having a hard time getting out of the house."

"I see," you respond. "You're telling me things are kind of crazy on your end and a bit of a challenge. Is that the case?" The dialogue continues in that manner, and you make no assumptions and say nothing to make Jerry defensive. You're just engaging in conversation, but eventually he tells you enough so that you know how to proceed.

In essence, you are taking the high road as you try to determine whether Jerry is on board with the company or not. You start by assuming the best. If it's just a temporary struggle at home, you will soon find out through your gentle questioning. He's trying. He wants to be productive. You can work with someone like that. You can help him overcome the problem. Or you may learn that Jerry has just ceased caring. He snaps at you for picking on him and insists his tardiness doesn't matter. Your approach then will be quite different.

OUT OF THE DARKNESS

When we started working together at the school, we often heard complaints from the ranks that they were kept in the dark. In response, the leadership put together glossy folders and programs and conducted hour-and-a-half information sessions on various topics of concern. In short, we went overboard. Many of the employees didn't want all those details. They wanted their leaders to be open with them about the big picture on a regular basis.

Think of it this way. If you plan to paint the hallway, will your employees care very much about how you choose the brand of paint, whom you will hire as the contractor, or whether the brushes and rollers are premium quality? Or will they just want to know what color it will be and when the painting will occur?

Supervisors need to understand how much information their employees want and need to know. If you tell your employees too much, you waste their time and yours. If you tell them too little, they may suspect that you are keeping them out of the loop. Not everybody will feel the same way, of course. Some employees thrive on all that talking. They want the details, and they want to know how you and everyone else feels about it all. Others just want you to tell them what they are supposed to do and then get out of their way so they can do it. They want effective communication, not excessive communication.

It's a shifting balance that requires sensitivity on the part of supervisors. Generally, it is better to share information and allow your employees to sort through what is most significant to them in being able to do their job. You create an atmosphere of secrecy when you withhold important information—or commonly known information. The outdated philosophy of sharing information only on a "need-to-know basis" will simply breed mistrust. Employees are experts at seeing through that game.

A much better approach is to share with them whatever you believe they might want to know. Make that the priority over what you think they need to know. Let's say your organization is changing a key strategy. You realize the importance of letting the employees know—but you also recognize that not everyone will want the same amount of background and all the details.

To strike that balance, you can set up a meeting with the employees where you give them the short story and the bottom line. At the same time, you offer them a document that includes all the details. The document itself will be divided into sections on various aspects of the new project that will be of interest to different groups of employees. Some might want to delve into the technological innovations of a new project, for example, while others only want to hear about the financial aspects. The nitty-gritty, in its various forms, is there for anyone who wants it. Anyone who doesn't want it can ignore it.

In short, when in doubt, share more, not less—and share continuously. That's how you build trust and a sense of culture. Instead of withholding information and making decisions for your employees about what they need to know, give them the details and let them decide for themselves how much they want. In that way, you communicate that you value their discretion.

If you want to create a culture of paranoia, you can instead do what many organizations have done: Hire somebody to come in and do a culture assessment and survey, interviewing staff at every level, and then never share the results with your employees. What is there to hide? If the survey points to areas for improvement, are you not all in this together? If you go to the trouble of commissioning a fifty-page report, then you should at least summarize the key issues to your employees in a half-hour presentation and offer them the full report for the asking. If you tell them nothing, then they will guess at what it says. You will be far better off if you are open about it.

Yes, some information is sensitive and confidential, but most is not. Most employees will understand and accept that you sometimes will be in possession of information that is not for dissemination. Tell them that. Reassure them that you would need a very good reason to keep anything from them. If you have been forthright with them over time, then they will trust you. Your track record is golden. You have engendered loyalty and commitment.

THE POWER OF SHARING

It is often stated that information is power, and that's true. Unfortunately, many leaders and supervisors hold on to information so that they can remain in control. They mistakenly believe that they will be viewed as the expert when they are the sole possessor of knowledge. Instead, employees typically see that type of leader as arrogant, mistrusting, and uncaring about the staff.

Leaders who hoard information as they try to maintain power tend to be the same ones who become irate with employees who do not share information with them. In other words, they exhibit a behavior that is very different from what they expect from others. That's not what you would call being a good role model.

Good supervisors lead by example. If you want your employees to be transparent, motivated, and concerned about the direction and success of your organization, then you need to become the respected role model for those behaviors and attitudes. You do that by building strong relationships. Camaraderie and loyalty grow as you get to know your employees as people, as they get to know you, and as they get to know one another.

You're not trying to be everyone's best friend. Rather, you are revealing yourself as a caring human being with a real life of your own. You are showing yourself to be a supervisor who is transparent and attentive. You are a leader who respects the employees enough to ask them to participate in decision making. If they are to do that right, you need to share what you know with them. Together you can build something better than anyone can accomplish alone—and that's the true spirit of "information is power."

Here are some things you can do to share continuously:

- Engage in regular feedback, both positive and negative.

- Actively listen.

- Be transparent.

- Avoid hidden agendas.

- Encourage two-way communication.

- Communicate generously.

- Share rationales for what you do or don't do.

- Share what is going on daily.

- Keep it simple and heartfelt, not technocratic.

- Respond with empathy.

Applying the principles:

- Choose an employee for a talk about his or her performance, whether good or in need of improvement.

- Outline how you will approach the conversation. Be specific about the issues you will address and the questions you will ask.

- Ask how you can support them in their continued growth and improvement.

"People will always work harder for something
they feel they have ownership of."

— PETER ECONOMY

CHAPTER 9

OPTIMIZING OWNERSHIP

Along with the importance of communicating effectively and sharing information, Coach taught the camp counselors that those most affected by a decision should be allowed to appropriately participate in making it. When people are involved in those decisions, he said, they will be more likely to accept and support them.

Coach pointed out, though, that it takes longer to make decisions that way. At other summer camps, counselor meetings usually took fifteen minutes to half an hour and were simply for sharing routine information about activities and events. Coach's meetings lasted an hour to an hour and a half, sometimes longer. Why? Because he involved the counselors in making the decisions about what they did and how. When they learned why Coach's meetings ran so long, the counselors from the other camps wanted to work with him the following summer.

It's 3:30 on a Friday afternoon, a half-hour before your employees expect to be heading out the door of your specialty machine shop. Wang, the lathe operator, needs to pick up his toddler from day care no later than 4:30. Frank, who works the drill press, has a dentist appointment at five. Orlando, the grinder, promised to take his wife out to dinner for their anniversary.

"Sorry, guys," you announce, "but we're all staying overtime tonight to get this order out, no exceptions. And everyone's coming in tomorrow morning for at least half a shift."

You already know what they're going to say because you've heard it all before: "So why are you waiting until now to tell us? If you knew we were getting behind, we could have put in the extra hours earlier in the week. We could have worked out a way together to get this done—but you didn't bother to ask, and now we're screwed." If they weren't saying that, they were thinking it.

You shrug and figure that if they want to keep their jobs, they will do as you say. You also know they are right. You knew you were in trouble, but you didn't ask them how they thought the company should handle this challenge. Now, they have to scramble to change their plans.

Had you talked to them in advance, they might have risen to the occasion. You could have appealed to their professional pride and motivated them to give it their all, and they no doubt would have appreciated the overtime pay. "Look, this is one of the year's biggest contracts, and we all know this will be tough to pull off, but if we blow this deadline we're not going to see it next year," you might have said. "What's the best way we could all pitch in to get it done by Friday?" Instead, you imposed your decision on them, and they feel no ownership in it. They look at you with contempt.

It happens all the time, particularly in the manufacturing world, where managers are prone to making such on-the-spot decisions when they are in a crunch—and it's murder on the employees. It's highly frustrating to have little say about matters that significantly influence not only your work life but also your personal and family life.

Suppose you supervise a department at a larger company and the word comes down via email that all budgets will be cut 10 percent or that a new vice president has been added who will now be your superior. Nobody tells you why. Nobody explains what the company is trying to achieve. Somebody made a decision without consulting the very people who must live with it. Why didn't you all get together to hash it out and decide what would make the most sense? It seems the leadership ignored a lot of smart people who could have offered some great ideas to benefit the company. If your superiors act as if they don't care about you, how much are you likely to care about the company? How much will you buy in to the mission?

Successful organizations will strive to optimize among their employees that feeling of ownership that motivates them to their best efforts. You put a lot of effort into hiring and training the best employees you could find. You invested a lot of time and resources. It's time now to claim your return on that investment. Involve your people in making decisions, solving problems, and dealing with other organizational challenges. With their abundance of talents and strengths, they very likely will have the answers that you need, and you should seek them out and trust them.

FOUR GENERATIONS IN THE WORKPLACE

How do you optimize ownership? You must be committed to engaging your employees by better understanding who they are and what they think, feel, and believe. You must appreciate the diversity on your workforce and the uniqueness of every individual. The first step is to gain a perspective and understanding of how they think and how they perceive the world.

For the first time in history, we are dealing with four unique generations in the workplace at the same time. Those generations show distinct preferences in what they want and need. Being involved will mean something different to each employee. Their expectations for job satisfaction will differ. To better engage them in their jobs so that they want to stay and help build your organization, you need to understand those preferences and adjust your approach.

This is not the first time that multiple generations have worked in the same environment. It has long been common, for example, for father, son, and grandpa to work together on the family farm or in the family store. What has changed in our times is the disparity in their outlook and values. Each generation has experienced a dramatically different world that has influenced their hopes, ambitions, and expectations in life.

Recently, we were chatting with a group that included baby boomers, Gen-Xers, and millennials. We began talking about whether high schools should use metal detectors for security. One of the millennials shrugged. He had experienced them and recognized the clear need. To him they were the norm. The older generations seemed appalled at the prospect. That's just one example of how the generations that are represented on your staff may view the world, and your work culture, differently. You will find many variations within each generation, of course. Though you must be careful not to label people, you can observe societal trends that will inform your style of leadership:

The traditionalists

Born before 1945, these employees represent only a small percent of the current workforce. Their core values include hard work, duty, and conformity, and they tend not to challenge authority.

They are dedicated and patient. They want respect for seniority. They respond well to a directive style of leadership and supervision. After years of loyalty, they want the gold watch.

The baby boomers

Born between 1945 and 1962, the boomers currently represent a larger percentage of the workforce; however, that percentage is decreasing dramatically. Their core values include teamwork along with personal growth and gratification. They are optimistic and involved, forever hopeful of a better world, and may be quick to challenge opposing views. They love to give feedback but may be overly sensitive when getting it and will want documentation. They make dedicated employees and respond well to directive supervision, although they prefer a more collaborative approach.

Generation X

Born between 1962 and 1982, the Gen-Xers represent a large percentage of the current workforce. Their core values include life balance and self-reliance. They don't define themselves by their job; they "work to live" rather than "live to work." They are technologically literate and think globally. They will be dedicated if they find their job rewarding and will seek out positive feedback to let them know whether they are on the right track. They don't do as well with negative feedback. They desire autonomy and thrive on recognition and appreciation. Their approach is informal, and they feel a job should be fun.

Generation Y (millennials)

Also called the "millennials," these are the employees born since 1982, who represent a rapidly increasing percentage of the current workforce. Their core values embrace a sense of civic duty and morality. They are realists who strive confidently to achieve and who love a challenge, and as such they make dedicated employees. They function well on teams. They look for constant feedback, to the point where they may misinterpret silence as disapproval. They want to know what they are doing right and what they are doing wrong. They are technologically demanding and expect information at the push of a button. In their fast-paced world, they are used to multitasking but may not take the time to listen carefully.

FOUR DISTINCT GENERATIONS

TRADITIONALIST *Born 1925-1945*	
	1927: Lindbergh's transatlantic flight
	1929: stock market crash (Black Friday)
	1930s: Great Depression
	1932: FDR's administration begins
SHARED EXPERIENCES	1939: World War II (start in Europe/United Kingdom)
	1941: Pearl Harbor (start of WWII in United States)
	1944: D-Day
	1945: victory in WWII
	1950s: Korean War

CORE VALUES	dedication/sacrifice
	hard work
	conformity
	law/order
	respect for authority
	patience
	duty
	honor
AT WORK	dedication/sacrifice
	tendency not to challenge authority or status quo
	"No news is good news."
	do not necessarily seek applause, but appreciate a subtle acknowledgement
	believe there should be a direct correlation between age and seniority/authority
	respond well to directive leadership/supervision
BABY BOOMERS *Born 1945-1962*	
SHARED EXPERIENCES	1954: McCarthy hearings
	1955: Rosa Parks & Vietnam
	1957: nuclear power plants
	1960: Kennedy administration
	1962: Cuban Missile Crisis
	1963: John F. Kennedy assassination
	1968: Martin Luther King assassination
	1969: Woodstock and man on moon
CORE VALUES	optimism
	teamwork
	personal gratification
	health and wellness
	personal growth
	youth
	work
	involvement / people skills

AT WORK	dedication/sacrifice
	prefer to receive feedback once or twice a year—need lots of documentation
	like to give feedback to others
	can be overly sensitive to criticism
	can be judgmental of those who see things differently
	although they respond well to directive supervision, tend to prefer a more supportive/collaborative approach

GENERATION X *Born 1962–1982*

SHARED EXPERIENCES	1970: Women's liberation
	1973: Watergate scandal and energy crisis
	1976: Apple computers marketed
	1978: Jonestown suicides
	1979: Three Mile Island
	1980: Ronald Reagan administration
	1986: Challenger explosion
	1989: fall of Berlin Wall
	1991: Desert Storm (Gulf War)
CORE VALUES	diversity
	global thinking
	balance (don't live to work)
	technology literate
	fun
	informal
	self-reliant
	pragmatic
AT WORK	dedication/sacrifice
	need positive feedback to let them know they are on the right track
	will ask for positive feedback when feeling insecure
	have difficult time with negative/constructive feedback
	tend to see work as "just a job"
	have a value for autonomy
	seek reward, recognition, and appreciation

GENERATION Y (MILLENNIALS) *Born 1982–2000*	
SHARED EXPERIENCES	1995: Oklahoma City bombings
	1997: Clinton/Lewinsky scandal
	1999: Columbine High School shooting
	2000: Microsoft lawsuit
	2001: dot-com bubble burst
	2001: September 11th attack on USA
	2003: invasion of Iraq
	2005: YouTube launched
	2007: IPhone released
	2008: Black Monday
	2008: Barack Obama elected president
CORE VALUES	realism
	civic duty
	confidence
	achievement
	sociability / electronic global community
	morality
	street smart
	technology demanding
AT WORK	dedication/sacrifice
	may fail to actively listen to older workers/supervisors
	feedback whenever at the push of a button
	may mistake silence for disapproval
	love a challenge
	need to know what they are doing right and what they are doing wrong
	function well in teams

STRATEGIES TO ENCOURAGE OWNERSHIP

With such disparity in the work styles of the four generations, how can a supervisor encourage all types of employees to do their best work—and to work well together? How do you instill the sense of ownership and pride that will energize the staff to excellence? The simple answer is that you should adjust your supervision style to match the employee. In today's age, it is no longer the employee's sole responsibility to adapt to the supervisor's style.

If you have traditionalists on your crew, for example, they probably will not be the type of folks whom you will call into a conference room every day to ask their opinions. That would just frustrate them. They would rather that you just tell them what you need them to do. They want your directions and instruction, and then they want you to get out of the way so they can do the job. Baby boomers, on the other hand, are eager for more involvement and want you to consult with them on how the job should be done.

Because everyone needs to do their fair share of the work, your job as supervisor is to find out what inspires them to be their most productive. You need to be consistent in your expectations, but you also should be flexible enough to account for individual needs. Here's a simple example. Let's say your organization offers three days of bereavement leave. One employee needs to travel across the country for a parent's funeral, while another only needs to go across town. Is an ironclad three-day policy fair to the employee who would have to spend the whole time traveling?

To be consistent in how you treat people does not mean acting as if they were stamped out of the same mold, living identical lives. You treat them fairly by acknowledging their different needs and skills and inclinations. You figure out where they will fit best on the team, establishing the roles in which everyone can make the most of their time and their competencies.

Let's look at some specific ways that you can optimize a sense of ownership in your workplace. None of them can stand alone; each depends on the others to be effective.

Involving employees in strategic planning

Strategic planning is not simply the purview of the leadership team. All of your employees should be involved in the brainstorming, and you should collaborate with them in major decision making. That way, they will see some of their own ideas incorporated in the strategic plan.

You need the perspective of those who will be performing the work. The leadership may think a task could be accomplished in two weeks, while the employees know from experience that it would take a month to do competently. Or perhaps they know they could finish in a week a task that the leadership believes would take a month.

The earlier you can involve the employees in the planning, the better. At the very least, send them a draft of the plan and ask whether you have missed anything. That will help to initiate a sense of ownership and buy-in. Each employee then can pay as much attention to the plan as he or she wishes. The traditionalists might not even look at it. The baby boomers probably will edit it. The Gen-Xers will examine it to see how it will impact them. And your Gen-Y people will ask whether you have considered new technology.

Encouraging appropriate risk taking

It often is good practice to let employees try something new, even if you suspect as their supervisor that it's not going to work.

So long as the idea will not be too expensive and detrimental to the organization, let them learn for themselves. When you create an atmosphere where taking appropriate risks is acceptable, you encourage initiative. Reassure your employees that it's okay to fail once on any project if they don't keep repeating the mistakes.

Empowering employees with new projects

When you allow your employees to take on new projects, you give them the opportunity to be truly proud of their work. Let them demonstrate their talents by giving them responsibilities that will showcase their areas of expertise. Because you have taken the time to get to know your employees as unique individuals, you will understand what excites them and the conditions under which they work best. You will be able to delegate to them the projects where they will shine. They will appreciate the challenge, and their success will boost their enthusiasm and lead to even greater accomplishments. You have hired a staff with diverse interests and abilities—so why not capitalize on those talents?

A COMMITMENT TO GROWTH

It is through open communication and empathy that servant leaders can fill their employees with a sense of ownership. Servant leaders don't dictate decisions but instead encourage staff members to share their insights, listening carefully to their ideas and creating opportunities for them to contribute and feel a part of the organization.

The servant leadership style promotes both personal and organizational growth. Employees who feel valued become much more engaged in their work. Satisfied employees work harder and more efficiently, and they don't run off in search of growth opportunities elsewhere. It's expensive to lose people you have trained and start anew. High turnover is a significant drag on profits—and, therefore, helping your staff to feel a sense of ownership will boost the bottom line. Organizations with engaged employees are able to soar ahead of the competition.

As a servant leader, you must be humble and willing to give up control. That is not the same as giving up responsibility. You remain ultimately in charge, but you can give your employees the opportunity to invest themselves in your organization. With your support, they will be able to take risks, learn new skills, and apply the many strengths and insights they already possess. They invariably will point you to solutions that you could not have discovered on your own. Don't think of yourself as the one with all the answers. Think of yourself as the one who knows where to get the answers.

Here are some things you can do to optimize ownership:

- Provide opportunities for staff to contribute.
- Link performance appraisals to the strategic plan.
- Create opportunities for healthy competition.
- Encourage participation with an open-door policy.
- Don't hoard power.
- Remind individuals of their value to the company.

- Encourage employees to take on new projects.

- Hold employees accountable even when you aren't there.

- Capitalize on your staff's many talents.

Applying the principles:

- Determine which generations are represented in those who directly report to you.

- Based on what you have learned in this chapter, develop strategies to build relationships and more effectively supervise them.

"Be patient with yourself. Self-growth is tender; it's holy ground. There's no greater investment."

— STEPHEN COVEY

CHAPTER 10

REALIGNING YOUR EFFORTS

Over the years, Coach constantly challenged the camp counselors to take an honest look at themselves and how well they were doing as servant leaders. In one way or another, he asked the same question repeatedly: "Would you want someone like yourself to be leading you in this situation?" It's a question that the counselors would be asking themselves in the years ahead as they evaluated their roles as husband, father, and friend.

On a return visit, one of those young men was chatting with his longtime mentor about his career challenges. He was already in a supervisory position and was disappointed with an employee for whom he'd had high hopes. He was thinking of letting the employee go.

Coach listened carefully before responding. "You've told me a lot about what this guy has been doing wrong," he finally said, "but I'm more interested in knowing what you've been doing since you hired him to make sure he can do what you expect of him. Are you really helping him to be successful?"

"Isn't he responsible for his own success?" the young man asked, puzzled.

"Yes and no," Coach said. "I've found that when an employee fails, it's usually something the supervisor has done, or hasn't done, that led to it." The young man conceded that

he hadn't provided sufficient training and resources—but the damage was done. It was too late.

Coach's lesson is a good one for all leaders, both on the job and off. Are you doing all you can to help people succeed? If you are unsure, then ask them. You will probably hear some good ideas on how you can change to better support them, professionally and personally.

Up until now, we have been focusing on what you can do as a servant leader to support those you serve, the people who report directly to you. In this chapter, we will examine what you can do as a servant leader to serve and support yourself.

All leaders must evaluate themselves and set goals to strengthen the areas where they recognize weaknesses and to further grow their strengths. How are you doing as a supervisor? That's a question you should be continuously asking yourself. How can you be better at what you do? What changes do you need to make?

Take a good look at yourself. If you were one of your employees, is this the person you would be proud to call your supervisor? If you can honestly identify some flaws and are willing to change your ways, then it's time for a tune-up so that you can better fulfill your role. You need to realign your efforts to meet the needs of your staff and your organization.

WHAT MAKES YOU TICK?

In addition to your self-assessment, you can also seek feedback from others in various ways. The most obvious is to directly ask them how you are doing as a supervisor. Either one-on-one or in groups, meet with your staff members to find out how well they feel you are meeting their needs and whether you could be doing anything else to better support them. A good question to ask is this: *What would you do differently if you were the supervisor?*

That's the informal approach to evaluating supervisory skills. You also can use a variety of professional assessment methods. We regularly work with individuals and teams to discover their strengths in such areas as problem solving, communication, conflict management, and other work habits and styles.

So that our clients can better determine where they stand, we have partnered with TTI Success Insights, a company that provides well-researched tools for measuring behavioral styles, as well as the training and support to use them effectively. The goal is to help organizations harness the talents and skills of their greatest asset, their people.

Those tools provide insights not only on how supervisors might improve but also on how team members can better understand one another's styles. The first step to improving yourself is to know what makes you tick. And when everyone understands the range of personalities on the team, they will be better able to adjust their own styles to accommodate and complement.

In one company, for example, some of the executives were getting frustrated with the president. They were all quick decision makers, the movers and shakers of the organization. The president, on the other hand, was a cautious thinker. When the executives came to her with what they felt was a great idea, they wanted her to act promptly. Instead, the president mulled it over a few days, considering the risks and looking at the big picture. Through professional assessment, the executives came to understand and appreciate how she operated. She wasn't taking her time because she didn't care. It was because she cared deeply.

These evaluations shed light on people's styles—their personality type, motivators, talents, strengths, etc.—but never is it a matter of right or wrong. You can be the polar opposite of someone on a personality assessment, for example, and still get along famously as colleagues and friends. Both of your perspectives are legitimate and valuable. The two of you might approach a situation and see two entirely different things—and neither of you would be wrong.

Consider the age-old tale of the three blind men who came upon an elephant. The first man approached it from the front and reached out to feel its trunk and tusks. The second approached it from the rear and grabbed its tail. The third came up to its side and rubbed its belly. Each of them described an encounter with an entirely different beast—and none of them got it wrong. They just didn't get the big picture until they compared notes. They were operating from a limited perspective. Or talk to two eyewitnesses of the same highway accident. You will get two different accounts. Neither is lying. They just had two views of the truth.

To be sensitive to other people's views is fundamental to good supervision, and that's why it pays to learn about your own perspectives. It's a good idea, as well, for you and your teammates to share what you learn about yourselves with one another. This is not information that you should keep to yourself. Only by sharing it will you attain a greater understanding. Again, it's not as if you are passing or failing some test. You are simply revealing where you fit in the continuum of humanity.

ASSESSMENT TOOLS

Let's take a look at some of the professional assessments from TTI Success Insights® that we use to help clients better understand who they are and how they might adjust their style of leadership to bring out the best in others.

Behaviors

Success in life, work, and relationships stems from having a sense of self—of deeply comprehending who you are, what you do, and how you do it. We use an assessment that measures behaviors based on the DISC theory first developed by William Moulton Marston. DISC measures Dominance, Influence, Steadiness, and Compliance.

This assessment is key in helping people to understand how they are inclined to behave and how they can interact effectively with others at work and in life. This understanding helps them to deal with problems and challenges, to influence and lead others effectively, to adjust to the pace of their environment, and to work well under established rules and procedures.

Motivators

Whereas the behaviors assessment illustrates the "how" of your actions and decision making, this assessment, based on Eduard Spranger's theory of human motivation, explains the "why" behind your actions and passions. Motivators are the windows through which an individual views the world. They are the driving forces that influence on-the-job performance, and they explain a lot about why an employee acts a certain way.

The assessment measures the relative prominence of six basic interests or motivators. Basically, these are fundamental life values:

- theoretical—the discovery of truth

- utilitarian—ROI of one's time and resources

- aesthetic—form and harmony

- social—an inherent caring for people; helping others

- individualistic—personal power, influence, and renown

- traditional—a system for living

Competencies

For many jobs, it's not always the technical skills that will catapult employees to success but rather the personal skills or "soft skills," which often are transferable to different jobs. In the workplace, technical knowledge is complemented by such intangible skills as leadership, persuasion, and playing well with others. These are qualities that define us as people. Typically, they will be key to an employee's job performance.

We can measure competencies with an assessment that examines the level of development of twenty-five unique personal skills. Those can be ranked from the most well-developed skill to the one in greatest need of further development. Different jobs, of course, require different competencies. Here are the personal skills that the assessment examines:

1. Understanding others

2. Continuous learning

3. Employee development/coaching

4. Interpersonal skills

5. Leadership

6. Personal accountability

7. Decision making

8. Appreciating others

9. Influencing others

10. Negotiation

11. Self starting

12. Customer focus

13. Diplomacy

14. Problem solving

15. Resiliency

16. Goal orientation

17. Project management

18. Creativity and innovation

19. Futuristic thinking

20. Planning and organizing

21. Conceptual thinking

22. Flexibility

23. Time and priority management

24. Teamwork

25. Conflict management

Emotional Intelligence

To achieve superior performance in the workplace, you must understand the role of emotions—both your own and other people's—in

the decision-making process. That understanding will lead to greater collaboration and boost productivity.

Research shows that successful leaders and superior performers have well-developed emotional intelligence skills. This makes it possible for them to work well with a wide variety of people and to respond effectively to the rapidly changing conditions in the business world. In fact, a person's (EQ) emotional intelligence may be a better predictor of success performance than intelligence (IQ).

The EQ assessment we use examines five key areas:

- self-awareness—understanding one's moods, emotions, and drives and how they affect others

- self-regulation—ability to control or redirect disruptive impulses and moods; to think before acting

- motivation—passion to work for reasons beyond money or status; pursuit of goals with energy and persistence

- empathy—ability to understand the emotional makeup of other people

- social skills—proficiency in managing relationships and building networks

OTHER MEANS OF ASSESSING SUCCESS

We also make use of two other assessments that TTI has developed—Job Benchmarking, which defines the parameters of a position, and the 360-Degree Feedback Survey, which goes full circle in gathering appraisals.

Hiring often is based on subjective perspectives and opinions. Job Benchmarking is a system by which you can define the key focus areas for every position. You do so by gathering several people who truly understand the position. Each of them knows intimately what the job entails—and each then takes the assessments on behaviors, motivators, and competencies. They respond to the assessment as if "the job was talking"—and their responses can be compiled into what amounts to a profile, or benchmark, of the kind of person who would be best for the job. Then, when the list of candidates is narrowed to a few, the finalists take the assessment. By comparing the results to the benchmark, you can get valuable insight into whom you should hire.

The benchmarking makes a hiring process more objective, basing the decision on data rather than feelings. In addition, as you begin to coach the person you hire, you can use the benchmark to point out areas of strength as well as areas that might need further development. You will not need to wait several months to start working on those matters as they become apparent. You can hit the ground running on day one.

The 360-Degree Feedback Survey is an appraisal tool to gather the observations of the employee's supervisor, peers, and those who report to him or her. They weigh in anonymously on a range of workplace competencies and behaviors, rating the employee on a scale and also offering written comments. As a development tool, the survey helps employees recognize their strengths and weaknesses so that they work more effectively.

Ultimately, a good measure of your success is how well those you serve are succeeding. In other words, are those you supervise meeting their own goals, as well as those of the organization?

What is the turnover rate of employees within your department? You need to get the "right people on the bus," to borrow a phrase from management consultant Jim Collins. And they need to be in the right seats. If you have done that well, they will be succeeding—and so will you.

YOUR BEST SELF

Now that you know the importance of developing yourself as well as those you supervise, what are you going to do with that information? How are you going to reinvent yourself into a more effective servant leader?

As we have shown throughout these chapters, servant leadership can be achieved by emphasizing such concepts as vision and engagement. You build it by developing relationships and focusing on values. Those are the means by which you can evolve into a strong leader who sees service to others as the prime directive.

Some leaders would rather attend to everyday tasks than engage in creative visioning. They choose to stick to the duties at hand. Other leaders would rather dream than get bogged down with what they considered to be the mundane. Effective servant leadership requires a good balance. Attending to the duties advances the dream. The dream makes the duties meaningful. Regardless of your inclinations, you can do both if you set your mind to it.

Their holistic attitude sets servant leaders apart from others. They are consistent in how they treat others and what they expect. They deal well with the conflict that inevitably will arise in the workplace, using their listening and empathy skills to resolve challenging issues. In fact, they see that conflict as potentially healthy, if everyone can reflect on it appropriately. It can stimulate growth.

Servant leaders work to promote awareness, and they know that comes from continually enhancing their knowledge and sharing it. They understand that they must get to know those they lead because their personal lives and their work lives are inextricably connected. Through the development of strong relationships, employees come to feel truly a part of the organizational community.

Those are the ways in which a servant leader functions in the workplace. As you strive to improve, those will be some of the qualities you develop. Along the way, it is critical that you take precious time to evaluate yourself. Look inward with honesty. Examine your strengths and weaknesses. Make the most of what you do best—and do your best to improve the rest.

Here are some things you can do to realign your efforts:

- Evaluate yourself as a supervisor daily.

- Highlight your abilities and potential.

- Don't jump to conclusions.

- Ask for feedback and reflect on how you could grow.

- Refocus on those you serve.

- Collaborate on decisions.

- Explain decisions and listen carefully to responses.

- Act consistently with what you require of your staff.

- Map out the goals you set for yourself.

- Step outside your comfort zone.

- Assess your style.

Applying the principles:

- Based on a professional assessment, write down three areas where you are strong and three areas where you need to improve as a supervisor.

- Meet with employees to gather their views on how you are doing as a supervisor—both the positives and the negatives. Does their assessment match yours?

- Use what you have learned to enhance your supervisory skills. Capitalize on your strengths and improve any weak areas.

*"Experience is not what happens to a man; it is what
a man does with what happens to him."*

—ALDOUS HUXLEY

A DEVELOPMENTAL APPROACH

Alone in his car after Coach's funeral, the man reflected on all that his old mentor had meant to him in their many years together at the Poconos summer camp. Coach had instilled in him the heart of a servant leader—and that summer, as the camp's new head counselor, he would be put to the test. He was heading back there now to fulfill his duties, and as he drove he whispered a prayer: "Lord, help me to be the kind of servant leader for the others that Coach always was for me."

As he reminisced, the man realized that what he believed to be true about leadership was the culmination of those years of faithful mentoring. Still a teenager when he began working at the camp, he had felt safe in taking risks and learning new skills. As the years went by, Coach allowed him greater flexibility in keeping with his experience and proven abilities, helping him to gain the motivation, autonomy, and self-awareness that he would need for such a time as this.

Closer now to the camp, he recalled the final lesson that Coach had shared with him the last time they were together, just before the camp season had begun. Coach warned him that as head counselor there would be days when he would feel overwhelmed trying to be everywhere at the same time and everything to everybody. "When you feel that way," he said, looking at his protégé the way he did when he was about to share some wisdom, "take some time to yourself every day or so and go off to a quiet place, or take a nap. The world won't crumble without you for an hour, and you'll learn not to take yourself so seriously."

As he turned into the camp, the man felt that he had found that quiet place. He felt re-energized now, eager for the challenge ahead. His heart was filled with gratitude and the desire to give back. And he knew then the most valuable lesson that his mentor had taught him: lead by example, and lead from the heart. That was Coach's legacy, and he would carry it with him for a lifetime.

If you want to be a good supervisor, you should learn what it's like to be supervised—particularly by someone with the heart of a servant leader. You need to acquire the necessary knowledge and skills to manage others, certainly, but you need a whole lot more, and that's what you will get when you are mentored by a pro.

An experienced servant leader will guide you along your path and help you to grow, giving you abundant training and support at every step. He or she will meet you wherever you are on that path, whether you are a beginner or well on your way, and get to know all about you, understanding that you will learn and advance in your own way and at your own pace. Under such guidance, you will mature and develop over time and gain the autonomy appropriate for your level of experience.

Servant leaders consider your success to be a measure of their own success. And when you do succeed, and you have assumed the role of supervisor yourself, then you can begin to give back. You can mentor others in the art of supervising from the heart. Understand that you still will be growing, and that just like those you are coaching, you will be honing your own skills over time. You will advance from novice supervisor to expert supervisor, wise in the ways of leadership.

Never believe that you have learned all that there is to know. A good leader is not afraid to ask, "How am I doing?" The soldiers who have been out on the field can tell a thing or two to the young lieutenant fresh out of the academy. Seek out the wisdom of those you serve and incorporate it into your style as you lead by example. When you respect their experience and expertise, they will respect your guidance.

As a servant leader, your job is to create a safe atmosphere where ideas and concerns will flow openly. Your role is to coach. It's not about you. It's about the others on your team and in your world. You are the catalyst for learning and growth. Your role is to facilitate success for those you have the privilege of supervising and for the organization whose values and mission you endorse.

Ultimately, you are serving that organization and its interests, and productivity is paramount for survival in an ever more competitive world. Many supervisors focus so intently on the numbers, however, that they alienate and hurt people and thereby hurt themselves. The solution is to focus first on the people, then on productivity. Remember, your number-one job as a supervisor is to lead with your heart!

ABOUT RISING SUN CONSULTANTS

Rising Sun Consultants views all consulting opportunities from a holistic/systems approach. Focusing on our commitment to servant leadership, Rising Sun Consultants places strong emphasis on appropriate stakeholder involvement from the very first step. We believe that it is essential for any organization's success for them to focus on the growth and development of their people. It is our goal to serve organizations in creating, developing, and maintaining a culture which inspires and motivates people to reach new horizons—both personally and professionally.

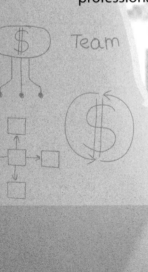

www.RisingSunConsultants.com